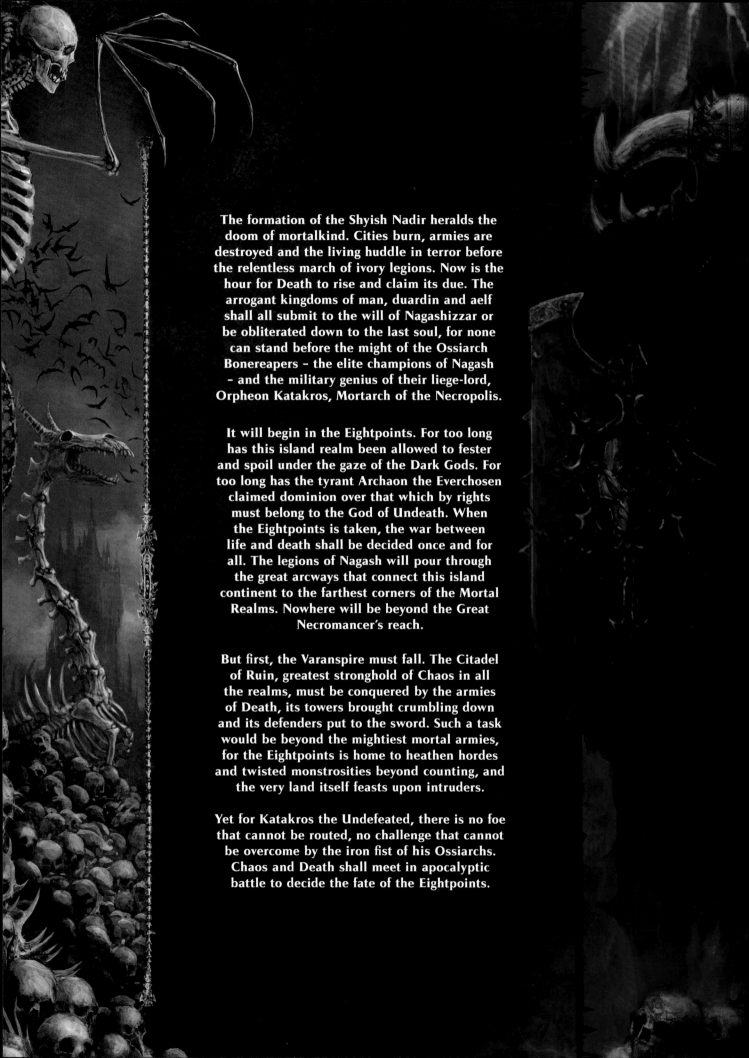

The formation of the Shyish Nadir heralds the doom of mortalkind. Cities burn, armies are destroyed and the living huddle in terror before the relentless march of ivory legions. Now is the hour for Death to rise and claim its due. The arrogant kingdoms of man, duardin and aelf shall all submit to the will of Nagashizzar or be obliterated down to the last soul, for none can stand before the might of the Ossiarch Bonereapers – the elite champions of Nagash – and the military genius of their liege-lord, Orpheon Katakros, Mortarch of the Necropolis.

It will begin in the Eightpoints. For too long has this island realm been allowed to fester and spoil under the gaze of the Dark Gods. For too long has the tyrant Archaon the Everchosen claimed dominion over that which by rights must belong to the God of Undeath. When the Eightpoints is taken, the war between life and death shall be decided once and for all. The legions of Nagash will pour through the great arcways that connect this island continent to the farthest corners of the Mortal Realms. Nowhere will be beyond the Great Necromancer's reach.

But first, the Varanspire must fall. The Citadel of Ruin, greatest stronghold of Chaos in all the realms, must be conquered by the armies of Death, its towers brought crumbling down and its defenders put to the sword. Such a task would be beyond the mightiest mortal armies, for the Eightpoints is home to heathen hordes and twisted monstrosities beyond counting, and the very land itself feasts upon intruders.

Yet for Katakros the Undefeated, there is no foe that cannot be routed, no challenge that cannot be overcome by the iron fist of his Ossiarchs. Chaos and Death shall meet in apocalyptic battle to decide the fate of the Eightpoints.

CONTENTS

PRODUCED BY THE WARHAMMER STUDIO
With thanks to The Faithful for their additional playtesting services

Games Workshop Ltd., Willow Road, Lenton, Nottingham, NG7 2WS, United Kingdom
games-workshop.com

Death has come to the lands of the Varanspire. The armies of the Dark Gods must unite to force back the soul-construct legions of the Ossiarch Bonereapers – or else face disaster.

INTRODUCTION

Archaon the Everchosen has claimed dominion over the Eightpoints ever since his triumph in the Age of Chaos, assigning warlords to rule with an iron fist over its nightmarish wilds and its vital, realm-spanning arcways. Now that supremacy will be challenged like never before, for an ancient and deathless power is rising in the realms…

The tome you hold in your hands tells the next exciting chapter in the grand story of Warhammer Age of Sigmar. It is a dark time for the Mortal Realms. Nagash, God of Undeath, has unleashed the horror of the Shyish necroquake upon reality. Everywhere, darkness falls, and the Great Necromancer's armies march forth in untold numbers to enslave and destroy the living.

Greatest of all his weapons are the Ossiarch Bonereapers, relentless soul-constructs fashioned using the darkest necromantic magic and commanded by the unmatched military genius known as Katakros the Undefeated. Already they have conquered great swathes of territory, driving their enemies before them in panic and terror, demanding that defeated mortals provide them with a tithe of fresh

bone with which they will construct more of their kind. Yet Nagash has even greater ambitions in mind. He seeks to conquer the Eightpoints, stronghold of Chaos in the Mortal Realms and the throne of Archaon the Everchosen, his hated foe. Should he succeed in this ambitious plan, Nagash would gain control of the arcways – immense arcane gates that connect the Eightpoints to each of the realms. Then, his war of obliteration could truly begin in earnest.

Victory will not come easily. The Eightpoints are home to vast warhordes sworn to the Dark Gods, their ranks consisting of the most vicious and bloodthirsty killers to be found anywhere in the realms. Furthermore, Archaon can call upon daemonic legions from the roiling hellscape of the Realm of Chaos

as well as fanatical murder-cults, mutated, flesh-eating monsters and even the predatory malevolence of the land itself. The Three-Eyed King is as formidable a conqueror as Mortarch Katakros, responsible for the obliteration of countless kingdoms and the enslavement of millions of defeated foes. Armed with the Slayer of Kings and riding his daemon mount, Dorghar, Archaon presents an all but insurmountable threat to any foe – including the mighty Katakros and his conquering armies.

So begins the Siege of the Eightpoints, a cataclysmic conflict between Chaos and Death that will drown the Eightpoints in blood and fire. In a series of horrific battles, the fate of this vast continent will be decided – and perhaps that of the Mortal Realms themselves.

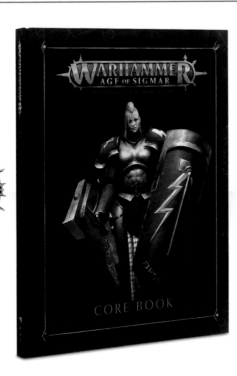

WARHAMMER AGE OF SIGMAR CORE BOOK

The rules in this book are intended to be used with the *Warhammer Age of Sigmar Core Book*. This tome is your ultimate guide to the vibrant fantasy universe of Warhammer Age of Sigmar. Within its pages, you will read of the troubled history of the Mortal Realms, from the glorious days of the Age of Myth, through the carnage and strife of the Age of Chaos, to the emergence of the Stormcast Eternals and the deadly events of the Shyish necroquake. Reams of exciting narrative and beautiful art will immerse you in this world like never before and provide endless inspiration for your hobby.

Each of the Eight Realms is covered in great detail, and in-depth background and stunning maps are provided for key regions in the realms of Fire, Life, Death and Metal – the areas most fiercely contested by the God-King's armies and those of his greatest enemies.

When you are ready to lead your forces to battle, you will find the core rules for the game, including multiple ways to play and additional, optional rules to enhance your experience. So gather your armies and take up arms, for the fate of the Mortal Realms is yours to decide!

MUSTER YOUR ARMIES

On the following pages, you will read of the full scale and horror of this massive conflict. A detailed history of Mortarch Katakros' grand campaign will describe the major battles that took place, the motivations of the key commanders and generals on both sides, and the ramifications of each fateful twist and turn in the escalating slaughter.

As well as an exciting, fast-paced story that advances the grand narrative of the Age of Sigmar, you will find everything you need to recreate the deadly struggle for the Eightpoints in your own games of Warhammer Age of Sigmar.

Unique battleplans will allow you to restage the most climactic battles of the Siege of the Eightpoints upon the tabletop, leading your armies through every brutal ambush and bloody, close-quarters skirmish as you take on the role of the greatest military minds in the Mortal Realms. Though these battleplans are primarily intended to re-enact the struggle between Chaos and Death detailed in this book, they also represent archetypal conflicts that have played out across the Mortal Realms. This means that you are free, if you wish, to use your own models and collections to rewrite history, taking the stories provided in this book as inspiration for your own heroic struggles.

These battleplans are presented alongside full realmscape rules designed to recreate the horrifying conditions experienced by those fighting amidst the twisted and corrupted wilds of the Varanspire. Also included are unique mechanics that introduce untamed endless spells into your games, as well as rules governing the wandering horrors that inhabit the Varanspire – these ferocious creatures can turn upon your own forces as easily as your enemy's, transforming any battle into a wild and unpredictable affair.

Rules for siege battles allow you to recreate your own brutal struggles to destroy or protect a fortified stronghold. Using these guidelines, you can either designate a set of terrain features to be your fortress and defend it against all who would seek to breach its walls, or you can take on the role of attacker and reduce your opponent's citadel to rubble.

Finally, you will find a selection of unique command traits, artefacts of power and abilities that allow you to represent the various Chaos hosts and daemonic forces doing battle against the armies of Katakros. Also included are warscroll battalions for the Legion of Chaos Ascendant – a vast gathering of daemons fighting under the banners of the united Dark Gods.

So whether you wish to take on the role of the conquering general Katakros, to wield the blazing sword of the Everchosen, or to tell your own story of battle and bloodshed amidst the wild lands of the Eightpoints, this book will allow you to live out one exciting battle after another. Take up your arms, raise your banners and lead your warriors to glorious victory in the name of the gods!

AN AGE OF STRIFE

It is a time of conflict and disruption in the Mortal Realms. Great powers find their dominance threatened on multiple fronts, while nascent powers rise to challenge the established order. War touches every corner of reality, and change is both violent and constant.

Since the dawn of the Age of Sigmar, the Mortal Realms have known little but constant war. Great cities of the God-King may have risen to prominence in Aqshy, Ghyran and beyond, but the wolves have ever howled at their door, desperate to feast upon the thousands of souls sheltered behind their strong walls and fortified gatehouses. Founded in the aftermath of the Realmgate Wars – that climactic conflict for the control of key arcane pathways between the realms – the Cities of Sigmar have endured only thanks to the sacrifice of countless lives.

Yet those long years of hardship and conflict have been dwarfed by the magnitude of events beyond the borders of the God-King's empire. Nagash, Supreme Lord of Undeath, has worked his greatest and most terrible spell, reversing the flow of magic in the Realm of Death and birthing the all-devouring abyss known as the Shyish Nadir at its heart. The aftershock of this momentous event – the necroquake, as it is known by many – has touched every corner of the realms, sundering the laws of magic and dragging hosts of vengeful spirits up from the underworlds. Ravenous, predatory spells roam at will. Furious aetherstorms surge across the skies, whipping up cyclones of raw magic that savage cities and frontier townships. Illusions and enchantments that have held for centuries have been shattered by the great unmaking, unleashing ancient monsters and curses long forgotten upon the realms.

Nothing is as it was. Whatever fragile balance of power once existed has been thrown into disarray as mighty empires are stricken by crisis after crisis and nascent kingdoms rise to feast upon the scraps of their shattered hegemony. With strife comes opportunity, and ambitious powers seek to increase their gains through the destruction of their rivals. In the midst of such unpredictable change, only one thing remains certain: undeath is in the ascendancy. Nagash has finally cast aside any pretension of an alliance with Sigmar, his one-time ally, and has enacted his own plans for supremacy over the realms. From his capital of Nagashizzar, the Great Necromancer plots the destruction of all life and the rise of a new, undead order.

As his Nighthaunt armies sweep across the realms, spreading fear and panic like a sickness, so too does Nagash unleash his corporeal forces – Deathrattle barrow-armies, the great legions of his Mortarch generals and darker things besides. His power seems limitless. Many free cities have been overwhelmed by a tide of rotting flesh and bone, their populace put to the sword and then raised by necromantic magic to fight on behalf of the God of Undeath.

It is not only the armies of the God-King that are suffering at the hands of a resurgent Nagashizzar. Though the forces of Chaos still claim dominion over vast territories and have earned a number of significant victories against their many foes, the sheer momentum of Sigmar's offensives has loosened their iron grasp upon the realms. In the manner of sprawling, decentralised empires throughout history, the mortal armies of the Dark Gods are being assailed on multiple fronts. Already embroiled in grinding wars of attrition against the God-King's forces and plagued by a drastic increase in greenskin raids, they now find themselves swarmed by spectral horrors and shambling hordes of risen dead.

The fortified sub-realm of the Eightpoints lies at the very centre of the cosmos, equidistant from each of the Eight Realms. Connected to these distant lands by immense arcway portals, it is a strategic location of unmatched importance and the domain of Archaon the Everchosen, Exalted Grand Marshal of Chaos. Here can be found his stronghold, the Varanspire – a monumental fortress-citadel haloed by a swirling crown of infernal magic that spills the raw, protean energy of Chaos into reality.

Archaon is perhaps the most feared military commander in the Mortal Realms, but he is not omnipotent. Such were the gains made during the Age of Chaos that the regions under his control are unthinkably vast, stretching into every realm save Azyr. Yet the loss of many important transitory routes during the Realmgate Wars greatly impacted on the Everchosen's ability to redirect his hordes across such distances in an instant. This left many important Chaos fiefdoms isolated, forced to fight on alone in the face of terrible odds.

Still, only a fool would question the dominance of the Dark Gods in the Mortal Realms. Sigmar's great cities occupy but a small bridgehead in a near-infinite expanse of territory. While the Eightpoints and the Varanspire still stand, the armies of the Everchosen cannot truly be defeated, and the threat of their dark crusades will always loom on the horizon.

ANARCHY AND TYRANNY

The Great Necromancer's hatred for the anarchic passion of Chaos is cold and everlasting. Nagash would no sooner ally with the warlords of the Dark Gods against Sigmar than he would seek alliance with the mercurial Idoneth or the scuttling tides of the Gloomspite.

To a creature driven by cold and implacable logic, who thrives upon exacting precise control over every minute detail of his lifeless empire, the unpredictable and savage emotions of Chaos are truly anathema. The Great Necromancer knows there can be no true order or peace in the realms until such emotions are purged, banished along with the deities that feed upon them like parasites. If Nagash is to attain his goals of uniting the realms entire through Death, Chaos must be broken just as completely

as Sigmar. Archaon the Everchosen and the Eightpoints must fall – though such a task is easier imagined than achieved.

The Age of Chaos saw much of Shyish despoiled by the Dark Gods as Nagash was forced to flee from their daemonic legions. At the Battle of Black Skies, Archaon himself cut down the Great Necromancer before the gates of Nagashizzar, and Nagash remembers well the bite of the Everchosen's dread sword, the Slayer of Kings. This outrage has not been forgotten, but there are also coldly practical reasons why the Great Necromancer has set his eye upon the throne of the Everchosen.

The Eightpoints, seat of Archaon's power, remains a strategically vital nexus, linking several realms to a single point in space and time. While several of the great arcway gates were shuttered or wrested from the hands

of Chaos during the Realmgate Wars, many remain active, including the Endgate, which leads to Nagash's own lands in Shyish. Every day, winding columns of Chaos Warriors and Marauders stomp through them on their way towards fresh conquests. If these gateways were seized and fortified by undead sentinels unfailingly loyal to Nagash, it would further strengthen his grasp upon the Mortal Realms.

To assault such a powerful stronghold without due preparation, however, would be an act of reckless foolishness. Even for Nagash's near-limitless legions, such a conquest would be tremendously costly, with no surety of success. But the Great Necromancer now has a potent weapon at his disposal. A loyal servant of old has lately returned to his court, a being whose mastery of the battlefield perhaps exceeds even that of the Three-Eyed King…

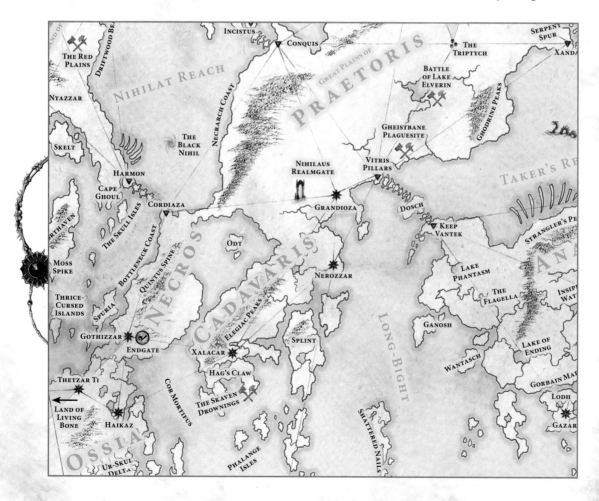

THE OSSIARCH LEGIONS

Ever a calculating and patient being, Nagash had begun to lay down the foundations of his rise to power during the Age of Myth. It was then – even while he paid lip service to Sigmar's pantheon – that the Great Necromancer began to create an army of conquest the like of which the realms had never before seen: the Ossiarch Bonereapers.

Fashioned from osseous matter and rendered soul fragments through the darkest necromantic rituals, these construct warriors were blessed with a flicker of sentience – a spark of autonomous thought that marked them from the charnel thralls favoured by lesser Deathmages. This made them truly terrifying foes, for while they possessed the relentlessness and utter loyalty of undead troops, they also boasted the strategic capability and skill of mortal soldiers. Before Nagash could test his baroque army upon the field of battle, however, the Dark Gods launched their great invasion of the Mortal Realms. The Age of Chaos dawned in blood and fire, and Nagash was driven into hiding in the underworld of Stygxx, his territories overrun by an endless tide of daemons. For many years, Nagash remained in hiding, reconstituting his power and preparing for the day when he would

return to regain control of Shyish and wreak his vengeance upon the Dark Gods and their puppet-king Archaon. In all that time, the Ossiarch legions stood undiscovered and silent in the deep places of the earth, awaiting the command of their master.

It was only centuries later, when the God-King Sigmar sent forth his heavenly hosts into the Mortal Realms, that the Great Necromancer at last seized his moment. Taking advantage of the confusion and disarray that had spread among the forces of Chaos, he burst forth from his hidden lair at the head of a vast host, summoning gales of deathly magic that lashed through the ranks of his enemies. Utterly unprepared for the violent momentum of this assault, many Chaos warlords of Shyish were soon either slain or in full retreat. The Great Necromancer reclaimed his ancient throne at Nagashizzar, defeating those arrogant chieftains who had dared to set up camp in the ruins of the deathly citadel and wreathing their essence in agonising soulfire.

Even in those early days of reconquest, Nagash did not call upon his Ossiarch legions; instead, he relied upon the vast numbers of his Deadwalker hordes and the speed and terror-raids of

his Nighthaunt processions to overwhelm the fragmented Chaos hordes. The Ossiarchs remained secure within their necropolises, for Nagash sought to find a commander worthy of such an army before unveiling them in all their macabre splendour. He would not waste this most potent weapon.

RISE OF THE MORTARCH

The one soul that Nagash desired to lead the Ossiarch Bonereapers against his enemies had fought for the Great Necromancer long ago, but he had long been thought lost or destroyed. It would be Nagash's own actions that would restore his foremost general to the court of Nagashizzar, albeit unintentionally.

Though the creation of the Shyish Nadir was achieved according to Nagash's desires, his incredibly complex rituals and incantations were not completed without incident. Unbeknownst to Nagashizzar's watchful sentinels, agents of Chaos had corrupted Nagash's grand spell, causing the necroquake to destabilise the very foundations of magic across reality. Enchantments and illusions that had concealed the great mysteries of the realms for centuries were torn apart, revealing long-forgotten secrets.

CONSTRUCTS OF BONE

The Ossiarch Bonereapers are no simple graveyard chattel, nor can they be raised wholesale from mass graves like zombies or skeletal warriors. The magic that goes into constructing such beings is incredibly complex and is carried out by the Mortisan priesthood – expert bone-crafters and necromantic artisans who have been honoured by Nagash with the secrets of soul-crafting. To shape an Ossiarch warrior requires two things: potent souls, which must be rendered down and remade into a fitting animus for the construct, and large quantities of bone, from which a physical shell is crafted. This same process is also used to fashion bonewrought fortifications in the field and to restore damaged war machines.

In order to replenish their immense armies, the lords of the Ossiarch Bonereapers require an ever-greater supply of osseous matter. Some of this they take from the corpses of slain enemies, retrieved in great loads by the horror engines known as Gothizzar Harvesters. Yet the majority is gathered from those living settlements dominated by the Ossiarch legions. In exchange for their continued existence, these vassal states must provide their undead masters with terrifyingly exact shipments of mortal remains.

Foremost amongst these were the Stormvaults, repositories established by the God-King during the Age of Myth. These chambers were built to contain things far too powerful and dangerous to be allowed to imperil the Mortal Realms, including magical creatures of godlike might, cataclysmic devices and artefacts too valuable for Sigmar to destroy.

The Penumbral Engines that had shrouded these hidden vaults were overloaded by the magical onslaught of the necroquake. Suddenly, every dark secret the God-King had sought to conceal was exposed. To Nagash, the revelation of the Stormvaults was yet more proof of Sigmar's duplicity. His fury was further exacerbated when he sensed a familiar presence beneath the city of Lethis, one of the God-King's major strongholds in the Realm of Death. Hidden there was the lingering spirit of Katakros, Mortarch of the Necropolis, the greatest and most feared battlefield commander to ever bestride the realms.

Katakros had been a prodigy of war even in his mortal life, a strategic genius born to lead. So obsessed was he with the mastery of warfare that when Nagash offered him the gift of immortality, he gladly accepted. In death, he became the Great Necromancer's most feared general and the first of the Ossiarch Bonereapers. The Mortarch was thought destroyed by a vengeful Sigmar when Nagash refused to come to his aid against the armies of Chaos. In fact, the God-King had imprisoned the Mortarch in the Midnight Tomb, a Stormvault that lay below the Raven City.

Upon learning this, Nagash sent forth Lady Olynder, the spectral Mortarch of Grief, to break open Lethis and recover his servant. Though the Sacrosanct Chambers of the Anvils of the Heldenhammer led a spirited defence that saved the free city, they were unable to prevent Lady Olynder from cracking open the Midnight Tomb and releasing the raging soul of Katakros. This was the first act in what would become a potent military union between the commander of the Nighthaunts and the Mortarch of the Necropolis.

Leaving a trail of devastation in his wake, the bodiless spirit of the Mortarch of the Necropolis broke free of Lethis and returned to his master's side. There, he was remade in physical form, presented with the most potent artefacts of Nagashizzar and once more granted his title of 'the Undefeated'. Once again, he would take his position as Nagash's foremost military commander.

KATAKROS RESURGENT

No sooner had Katakros been restored to physical form and clad in his enchanted raiment of war than Nagash gave him command of the Ossiarch Bonereapers. At last, he might be revenged upon those who had humiliated him. The Mortarch of the Necropolis did not waste a moment before mobilising the full force of his legions for war. Rank upon rank of Mortek Guard marched forth from their ancient sepulchres, spears and bone armour gleaming, the glimmer of hateful sentience in their eyes. Wedge-shaped cavalry formations of undead riders and clattering war engines of gruesome construction supported these phalanxes of infantry. After observing this deployment with cold satisfaction, Katakros summoned his foremost commanders and issued them with precise and unequivocal orders.

First to be scoured would be the lands east of the Shyish Nadir, an imposing stretch of underworld continents together known as the Ossiarch Empire. This vast expanse had once been Katakros' domain, but in the years since his fall, old enemies had seized much of the territory. They were to be reminded of their place – and swiftly. The Ossiarch Bonereapers began a methodical purge of the tainted empire. Chaos tribes, corrupted duardin kingdoms and rampaging orruk warclans were all put to the sword, their remains providing further materials for the Mortisan priesthood. So too did Katakros delight in taking the war to the Stormcast Eternals, in whom he saw an intriguing new challenge to be overcome. Upon the banks of the raging Daxamatic River, he smashed the Greygaunts Chamber of the Anvils of the Heldenhammer, repaying for the first time – but not the last – his long years of captivity at the hands of the black-clad warriors.

In a matter of seasons, Katakros could claim unchallenged command over the old empire. More critically, his campaigns had accumulated thousands upon thousands of slain foes – a fine treasury of bone with which to forge yet more conquering warriors. The Ossiarchs' first military actions had been ruthlessly successful, but Katakros knew that a far greater challenge awaited him. Nagash, his master, desired to strike at the Eightpoints and unseat the Everchosen from his infernal throne. Katakros, who took great pleasure in solving the most fiendish strategic challenges, knew that this might well be his most difficult task yet.

There were eight entrances to the island sub-realm, each of which was guarded by an All-gate, an immense bastion designed to keep even the largest besieging armies at bay. Those controlled by Archaon had been fortified with hellish war machines, deathtraps and many thousands of fearsome Chaos Warriors, while the rest were either in the hands of other foes or unreachable. The most strategically viable was the Endgate of Shyish; though still controlled by the Everchosen, if captured, it would link the Realm of Death with the heart of the enemy's domain. However, even if Katakros were to seize the Endgate and pass through its shimmering portal, he would doubtless find yet another series of fortifications on the other side.

While he was confident that his Ossiarchs could force such a breach, Katakros feared they would then be surrounded, trapped by interlocking defensive walls and slowly ground to nothing. But the Mortarch could call upon allies that would not be so easily contained. He dispatched a skeletal messenger bird to Dolorum and the court of Lady Olynder, first mistress of the Nighthaunts.

As an impenetrable shroud of gloom and despair swept across the Eightpoints, the legions of Death marched forth to kill and conquer. Dread war-constructs, undead cavaliers and massed ranks of skull-faced infantry drove a path of ruin across the haunted wilds, faced at every turn by the mortal hordes of the Dark Gods, outraged at this intrusion into their domain.

DOMAIN OF ARCHAON

It was not only the holdings of the God-King that suffered greatly in the aftermath of the Shyish necroquake. Even the deadly wilds of the Eightpoints were ravaged by the after-effects of Nagash's great incantation, as the dead rose to prey upon the living and wrathful, sentient spells rampaged across the land.

The Eightpoints is the domain of Archaon the Everchosen and the heart of Chaos in the Mortal Realms. An enormous island situated in the centre of the cosmos and connected to each of the Eight Realms, this land mass has been thoroughly corrupted by the malign influence of the Dark Gods. Its population consists of savage, mutated monsters and roving warbands of marauders who seek to earn the Everchosen's favour through increasingly vile acts of sacrifice and murder.

It was not always so. During the Age of Myth, the Eightpoints was a centre of culture and commerce known as the Allpoints, a bastion of civilisation through which goods and travellers flooded from every corner of the realms. When the Age of Chaos dawned and Archaon the Everchosen led his armies to war against the God-King, the Allpoints was one of his most prized targets, for its strategic value was beyond compare. Situated on the borders of the continent were eight immense Realmgates – arcways that each led

to one of the Eight Realms. Thus was this strange land a nexus to all places, and whoever controlled it boasted untold power in trade and in war. The mighty civilisations of the Allpoints called upon the aid of the God-King's pantheon to construct defences on the other side of these arcways. Known as the All-gates, these citadels were each the size of a city, garrisoned by thousands of soldiers with defences unique to the realm in which they lay.

Many times Chaos hurled its numberless forces against the walls of the All-gates, but they could not prevail. Too proud and hateful of one another to unite, the Dark Gods each strove to claim the prize in their own name, employing their favoured strategies of subterfuge, disease or brute force without coordination. Only when Archaon claimed command of their armies and united the forces of Tzeentch, Khorne, Slaanesh and Nurgle beneath the sole banner of the Everchosen did the raw might of Chaos finally prove too much for the defenders. One by

one, the All-gates fell, and darkness spilled across the Allpoints. Grand cities and gleaming monuments were razed to the ground, millions of souls slaughtered and totems erected far and wide in honour of the Chaos pantheon.

In return for his triumph, Archaon claimed the Allpoints as his own domain, for he considered it a fitting stronghold from which to launch his fell crusades across reality. Enslaving millions of his captives along with the native population of Fomoroids – cyclopic builders who had formerly served the lords of the Allpoints – he began construction upon the Varanspire, his grand fortress. He also ordered the building of fortified highways leading to the conquered arcways, these themselves protected by interlocking formations of fortresses and watchtowers. Under his iron rule, the Allpoints was transformed into an infernal industrial and military powerhouse, and it was granted a new name that would echo in infamy across the realms – the Eightpoints.

THE EMPTY THRONE

The Varanspire is perhaps the mightiest fortress in the Eight Realms, rivalling even the God-King's great palace-city of of Sigmaron in terms of its vast scale and fearsome defences. So attuned is the Citadel of Ruin to the hellish tides of the Realm of Chaos that its interior obeys no natural laws – spiked walls seep the blood and tears of tormented victims, hallways collapse in upon themselves maddeningly and stairways stretch onwards into infinity. An unfortunate soul lost within its vaulted halls might accidentally stumble into the refracting nightmare of Tzeentch's Crystal Labyrinth or find themselves amongst the putrid furrows of Nurgle's Garden.

At the heart of the Varanspire lies the Chamber of the Vanquished. Here, amidst a forest of pillars carved with the screaming faces of defeated foes, stands a throne of flowing darkness. Forged from the souls of mythic figures slain by Archaon's own blade, this throne is always empty. It is said that the Three-Eyed King has sworn never to sit upon it until he has fulfilled his vision of conquest and dominated the entirety of the Mortal Realms in the name of the Dark Gods.

A LAND TRANSFORMED

Centuries on from its fall to Chaos, the Eightpoints is all but unrecognisable. None can truly picture the horror of such a place unless they are unfortunate enough to witness it for themselves. Vast expanses of tainted wilderness stretch as far as the eye can see, the very earth rippling and thrumming with the untapped power of Chaos. Warped beasts sweep across the plains on the hunt for flesh, their forms twisted nightmarishly by the touch of the Dark Gods. Totems and shrines of desecration line the horizon, littered with bloodstained trophies and the skinned hides of recent kills. The further one progresses towards the Varanspire, the more terrible the lands become. Infernal fusions of sinew and metal siphon cursed liquids from beneath the crust of the gore-stained earth. Tempests of scalding blood lash down from the bruised skies overhead, and swamps of molten flesh reach out with pseudopodic limbs to ensnare the unwary and drown them in their putrid embrace.

Sprawling slum-cities do exist beyond the walls of the Varanspire, but these are little safer than the tortured wilds. They are home only to the most deranged and sadistic of killers, dominated by warlords and Daemon Princes who govern through a combination of brutality and gleeful sadism. One can hardly walk ten paces through the streets of Chaos-ruled settlements such as Carngrad or Flayhaunt without stumbling over a tangle of butchered corpses or a luckless soul with their throat carved open, bleeding their last across the filth-strewn streets.

At the centre of the Eightpoints rises the Varanspire, the fortress of the Everchosen. Resembling a titanic sword thrust deep into the earth, this vast citadel of darkness stretches high into the sky and is crowned by a roiling portal of lurid shapes and colours – a gateway to the horrors of the Realm of Chaos. It is this portal that irradiates the land surrounding the Varanspire with the influence of the Dark Gods, and in times of war, the Everchosen can summon daemonic reinforcements directly from the domains of his patron gods.

During the Realmgate Wars, the forces of Sigmar led by the Stormcast Eternals managed – at terrible cost – to close the arcways to Ghyran and Aqshy, denying Archaon's forces passage to these two realms. All others save the Ghurish gate – located inside the roving monster Fangathrak – and the route to Azyr remained in the clutches of the Everchosen, who immediately set about expanding fortified Dreadholds around each arcway in the Eightpoints, tasking some of his most fearsome lieutenants with the responsibility of guarding them.

Perhaps greatest of these bastions was the fortress of Karheight, which guarded the mouth of the Endgate leading to Gothizzar in the Realm of Death. An immense edifice fashioned from cursed metal and reinforced by the darkest sorceries, this Dreadhold had been constructed to ensure that anything attacking through the Endgate would be immediately contained and destroyed.

Though Archaon's forces still held the Shyish side of the arcway, they had been subjected to an almost constant assault from Nagash's undead legions, a relentless campaign that showed no sign of abating. Well aware of the God of Undeath's megalomaniacal nature and utter hatred of Chaos, the Everchosen wished to ensure that should Gothizzar fall, his armies could withdraw to a second line of even more formidable defences on the other side of the portal.

VARANITE, THE MOLTEN REALMSTONE

Just as each of the Mortal Realms has its own unique form of realmstone, so too does the Eightpoints. Varanite – also known as bloodrock, octarite or Archaon's Gift – is a magical material suffused with the energies of Chaos that, in its natural state, resembles red-hot, bubbling gore. Varanite veins run in gushing channels below the crust of the Eightpoints, fed by the blood of the slain sinking into the earth and by the cascades of Chaos energy that spill from the portal above the Varanspire. To dip a single finger into the stuff is to find one's body overcome by mutation – in much the same manner as exposure to warpstone, though to a far greater and more unpredictable extent. When solidified through a hazardous process of extraction and sorcerous purification, Varanite can be forged into weapons of unspeakable power that do not merely carve open flesh, but also flood it with pure, unalloyed corruption. Even a slight wound will begin to reshape itself into horrific configurations; there are tales of weapons that cause razor-toothed mouths to sprout within the flesh of their victims and devour their host alive. The substance is so difficult and dangerous to mine that even the Everchosen's armies field few such blades, but each is the equal of a hundred lesser weapons.

ONSLAUGHT OF MAGIC

Though the Eightpoints was perhaps the most formidably fortified and garrisoned region of the realms outside of Azyrheim, the after-effects of the necroquake wrought terrible havoc within its borders. Raging deathstorms separated and isolated many of the Everchosen's legions and shattered key fortifications. At the great Dreadhold of Karheight, Chaos defenders felt the tremors of the realm-spanning disturbance shake the foundations of their fortress, splintering stone and sending more than one watchtower crumbling to the earth in a cloud of dust and shattered masonry. Screaming warriors flung themselves from the parapets in a vain attempt to escape the devastation. Fortunately, the Dreadhold itself – a star-shaped mass of cursed iron and invictunite that enclosed the Shyish arcway like a metal gauntlet – was too magnificent a structure to suffer such a fate. Yet all could feel the icy touch of death upon the air, chilling them to the bone. It was an omen of far worse to come.

It might seem impossible that such a place as the Eightpoints could grow any more terrible, but in the wake of the necroquake, that is precisely what happened. Packs of hateful Nighthaunts were dragged up from the underworlds in places rife with the energies of Death – and in the Eightpoints, such lodestones of slaughter were far from rare.

Though the miasma of Chaos magic that shrouded the Eightpoints seemed to keep at bay the vast processions of spectral dead that ravaged other realms, these smaller hosts were deadly enough in their own right. They struck at armoured columns and isolated warbands without warning, sweeping forth with blood-chilling screeches, raking at their living prey with incorporeal claws that froze the blood and stopped the heart. Such was the ferocity of the deathstorms – and the Nighthaunt attacks that inevitably followed – that they cut off entire regions of the Eightpoints, enveloping them in a squall of all but impenetrable amethyst magic.

But it was not solely the rising power of Death that brought ruin to the Eightpoints. Magical shock waves birthed by the trauma of the necroquake crashed across the realms, shattering established laws of magic and giving rise to conjurations beholden to no master and undiminished by the passing of time. Dragged through the arcways by violent aetherstorms, these manifestations of living magic swept into Archaon's realm by the score. The warping nature of the Eightpoints only exacerbated their furious power, giving rise to strange anomalies that made these spells as unpredictable as they were lethal. Flaming skulls swept along the ramparts of iron-pointed towers, immolating scores of luckless sentinels before splitting in two, each mirrored half embarking upon its own murderous spree. Lashing, spectral chains appeared apparently at random to ensnare entire warbands, dragging them off into the darkness. Purple Suns careened down the fortified roads of the Eightpoints, smashing through

column after column of Chaos Warriors and leaving screaming statues of crystal in their wake. Fissures in the ground that had become saturated by arcane power and Chaos energy vomited forth spells by the dozen, transforming entire regions into desolate wastelands ruled by untapped magic. Worse still, these living spells coalesced into hunting packs, drawn instinctively together to better bring ruin down upon their prey. The Everchosen's most powerful sorcerers could barely contain the rogue magics, and scores of lesser conjurers were slain in failed attempts to bind spells to their will. All who dwelt within Archaon's domain swiftly learnt to flee when they saw the blazing light of magic upon the horizon.

RIPE FOR DEATH

The Great Necromancer had not counted upon the lethal disturbances that were ravaging the Eightpoints, but he could hardly have planned a more successful disruption of his enemy's stronghold prior to his own invasion. As always, Archaon the Everchosen was absent from his dark throne, but this time he had taken the majority of his elite Varanguard with him. The Three-Eyed King's mission was of the utmost importance, a task that could be trusted to none other than the favoured general of the Dark Gods. The great lords of the Eightpoints would have to face the full might of Nagash's legions alone.

That is not to say that they would present an easy conquest. Command of the Varanspire garrison in Archaon's absence fell to the Chaos Lord Namon Saskarid. A cruelly ingenious castellan and veteran of the Bone Wars of Shyish, Saskarid had long battled against Nagash's armies at the Everchosen's side, and it was whispered that he would soon ascend to the ranks of the Varanguard. Saskarid's current task was no meagre one. In such turbulent times, any of the arcways could come under assault, and so all had to be safeguarded at all costs. From his warcamp at the foot of the Varanspire, Saskarid

attempted to organise a continent-spanning defence against potential threats, even as the Eightpoints was brutalised by the ongoing effects of the necroquake.

Only the Gaunt Summoner known as the Tongueless Lord sensed the concentration of amethyst magic gathering about the Shyish arcway. Serving as the vizier of Lord Saskarid in the Everchosen's absence, the mage-lord knew that if he failed to safeguard the Varanspire and its territories, Archaon's wrath would be immense. The Everchosen knew his true name, after all, and with such power he could tear the Gaunt Summoner's soul apart piece by piece.

From his Silver Tower, which hung alongside the spiked walls of the Varanspire, the Tongueless Lord worked his rituals and performed haruspicy upon the entrails of still-living prisoners. His attempts to divine the nature of the brewing disaster were stymied by the ongoing magical fluctuations, but his scrying crystals all focused upon Dreadhold Karheight at the far edge of the Corpse Wastes. The auguries of Death hung over that place like a funeral shroud. Immediately, he sent a psychopomp messenger to the court of Lord Saskarid, warning him to summon the hordes and make for the Shyish arcway in all haste.

Saskarid wasted no time. He ordered his coven of Sorcerers to burn the sigil of the Everchosen into the skies above Karheight. As the infernal rune blazed across the vast expanse of the Eightpoints, rival warbands across the continent

ceased their butchery at once, even those locked in brutal combat. Once more, they felt the inexorable call of the Everchosen summoning them to glory. Like moths drawn to a flame, they flocked towards the distant symbol and the promise of slaughter. Lord Saskarid mustered his elite guard of Chaos Knights, the Deathsworn, and hauled himself atop his Karkadrak mount. To the blaring of war-horns, the seneschal's retinue headed for Karheight.

From atop the spiked ramparts of Karheight, tattooed Marauders and grizzled Chaos Warriors looked across to the mist-shrouded silhouette of the Endgate, a circular portal that bled wan silver light into the Eightpoints. As they watched, its surface rippled and tore open, spilling forth many hundreds of bedraggled figures. These newcomers staggered forward, clad in furs and beaten iron marked with the eight-pointed star of Chaos. They made their way across the open ground towards the battlements of the Dreadhold, oblivious to the deadly hazards that lay before them. The stench of carrion filled the air. Every one of the Chaos Warriors stumbling through the arcway was dead, raised by necromantic magic to make war upon their former comrades.

The trenches stretching before Karheight in zigzagging lines were each filled with molten metal; many of the oncoming horde simply stumbled into these ditches and were instantly incinerated. Great sluiceworks built into the fortress wall spat flesh-melting liquid and screaming Marauders hurled axes and javelins down upon the mass of bodies as they lurched unwittingly into the spike-traps and killing pits littering the ground. Cheers and howls of laughter rang along the ramparts of the Dreadhold, but the more experienced Chaos Warriors knew that such cumbersome foes heralded the coming of something far worse. These zombies were the remnants of the Gothizzar garrison; and if they had been slain in such numbers, what form of massacre had taken place beyond the curling mists of the Shyish arcway?

ARCHAON THE EVERCHOSEN

Amongst the Champions of Chaos, Archaon stands alone. He is the Exalted Grand Marshal of the Apocalypse, the favoured of the pantheon, and by his command are the Mortal Realms remade in the image of Chaos. Behind him, the armies of the Ruinous Powers march as one, forged into a single terrifying force by the will of the Everchosen.

Every worshipper or beast of Chaos that walks, slithers or lopes owes obeisance to Archaon. He is less a man than he is a demigod of the Dark Powers, the chosen commander of their infernal hosts. Yet the Everchosen is no mere puppet. He has earned his position through might, cunning and a sheer determination that has seen the doom of entire worlds. Should the Chaos Gods ever achieve their conquest of the Mortal Realms, it will be in large part due to Archaon.

Archaon's origins are shrouded in mystery. Few are the souls who know the truth of his past. In the time of the world-that-was, Archaon bore a different name and fought as a devout templar of Sigmar. Upon reading the apocalyptic writings of the prophet Necrodomo, he learnt a terrible truth concerning the divinity of the Heldenhammer that shattered his every certainty. Taking the name Archaon, he swore to attain the mantle of Everchosen and take his vengeance upon his former lord. Across the realms, however, other tales have spread concerning Archaon. Some believe that he was a great Azyrite emperor who ruled before the coming of Sigmar and who swore himself to Chaos to match the power of the upstart God-King.

Many tribes believe that Archaon is a manifestation of the Dark Powers – that when Chaos came into being, so did their greatest champion. The tribes of the Untamed Beasts honour him as the Eater of Worlds, while the shadowy Corvus Cabal see him as an avatar of their avaricious daemon-god, the Great Gatherer.

Archaon's almighty status is demonstrated through his bearing of the legendary artefacts known as the Six Treasures of Chaos. These are no mere trinkets; each is an ancient item steeped in ruinous power that marks his status as Everchosen. Upon Archaon's brow burns the Mark of Chaos Ascendant, that rarest of sigils denoting the favour of all the gods. Within a groove upon the Crown of Domination sits the Eye of Sheerian, ripped from the belly of the Chaos Dragon known as Flamefang, which grants the Everchosen a degree of foresight – combined with Archaon's tactical brilliance, this makes him nearly impossible to outmanoeuvre in battle. The Armour of Morkar is almost impervious to enemy blows and was once worn by the first to bear the mantle of Everchosen in the depths of pre-history. Perhaps most infamous of these artefacts is the Slayer of Kings. Within this legendary blade is the essence of

the daemon U'zuhl, who delights in devouring the souls of monarchs and champions. Then, of course, there is Dorghar, the Everchosen's ferocious, daemonic steed.

Though he fights their wars and leads their armies, the Gods of Chaos regard Archaon with a measure of unease – perhaps even fear. They are right to do so. Each of the Brothers in Darkness has attempted to sway the Everchosen to their exclusive service and each has failed, the most powerful of their servants slain by Archaon or ripped apart by his monstrous mount, Dorghar. Within the abyssal reaches of his soul, there is a part of Archaon – or perhaps the man he once may have been – that looks upon the machinations of all deities, whether they are one of Sigmar's failed pantheon or his own supposed masters, with contempt. Many of those sworn to Chaos bear the Everchosen's brand above any of the dark pantheon. There are those who whisper that should Archaon ever achieve his ultimate aim of grinding the Mortal Realms beneath his heel, there will be no gods to play games with the lives of mortals – there will be nothing save the black banners of the Everchosen raised across the length and breadth of every realm.

DORGHAR, STEED OF THE APOCALYPSE

The fourth treasure claimed by the Everchosen was the daemonic steed known as Dorghar. The quest for this beast took Archaon into the Realm of Chaos itself, for Dorghar was once the most prized specimen in the menagerie of the daemon lord Agrammon. Infiltrating Agrammon's palace through cunning and guile, Archaon used the Eye of Sheerian to locate Dorghar's cage. Leaping onto the daemon's back, Archaon broke the creature in a titanic contest of wills, binding Dorghar through sheer force of personality – and by offering his new mount the chance to take bloody revenge on his gaolers. When the Gods of Chaos, save absent Slaanesh, sent some of the mightiest of their greater daemons to test the Everchosen's prowess, Archaon and his mount

soon shattered the challengers. Upon drinking the essence from their carcasses, Dorghar gained his three heads, each bearing the powers of one of the gods: the untrammelled rage of a Bloodthirster, the foetid sickness of a Great Unclean One and the sorcerous might of a Lord of Change. The fell sorcery that runs through Dorghar's veins also ensures that those he consumes never truly die, meaning that the Steed of the Apocalypse is particularly dreaded by the Stormcast Eternals. Those of their number devoured in battle by Dorghar – such as Thostos Bladestorm, Lord-Celestant of the Celestial Vindicators and hero of the Realmgate Wars – cannot return to Azyr to be reforged; instead, they are subjected to an eternity of torment in the creature's gullet.

TO FREE A GOD

Through guile and perseverance, Archaon the Everchosen had managed to locate the captive god Slaanesh, the Dark Prince of Pleasure. Held at the mercy of the aelven deities, Slaanesh was ensnared by godwrought chains, each of which could only be shattered by performing a deed of impossible difficulty.

Slaanesh, the depraved God of Excess, had been held captive by the aelf gods and their allies for many centuries, hidden away in some secretive realm so that the trillions of souls within his swollen belly – devoured during the cataclysmic destruction of the world-that-was – could slowly be freed from their torment. Archaon had long been determined to free Slaanesh. He had neither great fondness nor reverence for the Dark Prince, as he scorned all the gods equally, but he recognised the Chaos God's great power and how it could be turned towards his purpose. While Slaanesh was absent, a potent weapon was missing from the Everchosen's arsenal, and his fractious followers would continue to pursue their own debased ends – all to the detriment of Archaon's united vision of conquest and tyranny.

For that reason, he had assigned his most powerful arcane agents to discover the location of the Dark Prince's prison. Within their labyrinthine Silver Towers, his Gaunt Summoners had transcended physical form through sorcerous rituals, their astral essence roaming the cosmos in search of Slaanesh. For centuries, they found nothing but the tortured after-screams of agonised souls, refracted far across reality and impossible to trace. Someone, somewhere, was drawing power from Slaanesh on a grand scale, but the location of this transferral process remained well hidden. As the years went by, however, Archaon's spies and seers began to sense ripples in the fabric of the cosmos. Karanak, the three-headed hound of Khorne, was slain by daemonic servants of the Dark Prince, and the volcanic fury of the Blood God briefly tore at the illusions masking Slaanesh's prison. The massacres, infamies and disasters of the Shyish necroquake further frayed the complex web woven by the aelven gods. Alone, these events might have gone unnoticed, but together they formed a pattern of cosmic significance that manifested before Archaon in the form of a prophetic vision.

He saw Slaanesh bound in a prismatic prison between darkness and light, and he knew at once where the cunning aelves had hidden away the Dark Prince: in Uhl-Gysh, the twilight sub-realm that lay between the Realms of Shadow and Light. That was where he and his Varanguard would find their prize, but they would only have one opportunity to strike. As soon as Teclis and Tyrion realised their secret had been unveiled, they would surely drag the chained Slaanesh deeper into the shrouded pathways of the Hidden Gloaming and redouble their illusory wards.

BATTLE OF THE CHAIN

Like gleaming arrows, the Silver Towers pierced the twilight veil, puncturing the illusions of Uhl-Gysh and the warding enchantments Teclis had so painstakingly etched across the realmsphere. Ahead of the crystal monoliths loomed the shadow of a god. The bloated mass of Slaanesh appeared as a constellation of lurid colours and half-glimpsed atrocities, its shape impossible to ascertain, its aura one of abnormal yet tantalising horror.

As the Silver Towers descended, the amorphous god-essence shivered in anticipation, and soft laughter echoed across the Twilight Realm. The insubstantial, rippling mass of the Dark Prince was outlined by the gleaming lights of a dozen great towers of aetherquartz. They orbited the quivering entity upon isles of basalt. Sixty-six great chains stretched from the summit of these towers, arcing out towards the captive god and sinking into his intangible flesh. These were not chains of metal, for no physical material could bind a god. They

were instead formed from the purest shadow magic, woven from the umbral stuff of Ulgu itself.

Each god-chain was constructed and enchanted so that only one unique and paradoxical act could sunder it; thus, no single method could shatter multiple chains. As he looked upon the deity he had sought for so many years, Archaon the Everchosen gave a roar of triumph. Dorghar reared beneath its master, daemonic heads drooling in anticipation of the slaughter to come. Raising the Slayer of Kings high, the Everchosen urged his mount onwards and hurled himself from the Silver Tower, charging towards the uppermost aetherquartz spire.

Garrisons of white-armoured aelves were already spilling from the gates of the aetherquartz spires, arraying themselves in gleaming phalanxes, spears raised and shields locked in perfect synchronicity. Archers notched arrows, while sleek war machines raised their sights toward the oncoming doom. Teclis and Tyrion had assigned only their finest champions to the sacred duty of guarding the captive Slaanesh. Yet even these warriors could not halt the fury of the Everchosen. Archaon smashed Dorghar through the aelven line, and his elite Varanguard followed behind, the thundering hooves of their daemon mounts crushing aelven spearmen to bloody ruin. Silver Towers spat witchfire and unleashed flocks of screeching daemons, and the Gaunt Summoners turned their own sorcerous powers against the defenders of Uhl-Gysh.

Though the aelven guardians fought fiercely, the charge of the Varanguard could not be halted. Slaughtering his way to the summit of the spire, Archaon found himself at the foot of a great chain. Delighted laughter echoed over the thrash of battle as the Dark Prince looked upon his would-be rescuer.

At the end of a gleaming platform of polished marble was a great chain, formed by woven strands of umbral magic. It arced out into empty air, trailing across the twilit sky where it disappeared into inky blackness. The night rippled with lurid colour, and something impossibly vast stretched languorously, pulling the chain taut. The Everchosen could make out a form within the roiling sky – something sinuous and terribly beautiful, twisted in the contortions of infinite pain and pleasure.

Two blazing pools of violet light blinked open and fixed upon the Everchosen.

'So, you have come for me at last, dearling,' the Dark Prince said in a voice that rang out like a discordant note. 'I am touched.'

'I come for my purpose, not yours,' said the Everchosen.

'Always so bold,' Slaanesh purred. 'So… determined. My brothers have ever been suspicious of that, but I alone appreciate your single-mindedness. Some might even call it obsession.'

'I should leave you to rot here,' Archaon growled, angered by the god's insouciant air.

'Come now, we both know that you would not be so foolish. You need me, oh glorious Everchosen. Just as I need you. How I treasure our bond.'

Archaon stepped to the chain that stretched before him and drew the Slayer of Kings.

'Do you truly think so little of my captors?' sighed Slaanesh. 'Swords will not aid you here, not even your fine little blade. This is the Chain of Leashed Wrath. Only one of my brother Khorne's wrathful spawn may cleave it, and, as you know, he would never aid me willingly. I have tricked the dull-witted brute into doing my bidding once before, but even he is not so foolish as to fall for my deceit a second time.'

Archaon aimed the Slayer of Kings at the chain and a black comet struck from the sky. Dorghar, Steed of the Apocalypse, fell upon the shadow-links, grasping them between the teeth of its rightmost head, that which had once belonged to one of the fiercest of the Blood God's servants. It shook its sulphur-dripping jaws to and fro, and with a sound like shattering crystal, the wisps of twilight magic came apart.

Slaanesh groaned exultantly, the god's serpentine form shivering in delight.

'Oh, very well done, my beloved,' the Dark Prince hissed.

Archaon stepped forward, ready to swing himself up upon the back of Dorghar and seek out the next chain. Before he made it three paces, the Eye of Sheerian – embedded in Archaon's iron crown – flared, the sorcerous device sending a lance of agony through the Everchosen's skull. With the pain came a vision as stark as it was troubling.

He saw the Varanspire aflame and a shadow of death cast across the Empty Throne.

The Eightpoints was under attack.

LONG HAUNTED NIGHT

Mortarch Katakros' assault upon the Eightpoints commenced not with the lockstep march of Mortek legions but with the howling hatred of the spectral Nighthaunts. Uncontained by the physical defences arrayed by Chaos Lord Saskarid, hosts of cloaked horrors swept out of the Shyish arcway and fell upon the defenders of Karheight.

Even as the zombie horde clawed hopelessly at the walls of Karheight, the Shyish arcway once more rippled open behind them. An entire Nighthaunt procession poured out of the Endgate, rimefrost spreading before them and creeping across the parapets. These creatures feared no molten moats or iron-spiked barricades. They simply soared above such paltry, physical defences and surged towards their living prey, whom they despised with an intensity that turned the air deathly cold.

Rattling Chainrasps descended upon the defenders en masse, swiping away with rusted, incorporeal weapons that passed through armour and hide to stop the hearts of their victims. Bladegheist Revenants whirled and spun in a frantic dervish dance, dropping dozens of Marauders lifeless to the ground. Faceless nightmares drifted

eerily above the slaughter, drawing the choicest souls of the slain into their cursed padlocks. With every mortal essence so contained, nearby Nighthaunts seemed to swell with hateful power.

Victory was not assured. The Nighthaunts battled hardened warriors of the Eightpoints, many of whom had faced the wrath of the undying many times before. In this horde fought all manner of savage killers: murderous fiends from the Blood Bulls tribe, reaver champions of the Eyetakers, the gold-encrusted Gilded Ones and the flyblown zealots of the Putridae. Screaming prayers to the Dark Gods, these warriors of Chaos put aside their ancient hatred to drive the dead from their domain. Splattering trails of ectoplasmic matter flowed like blood as gheists were rent by cursed blades that tore through spirit-stuff as surely as if it had been mortal flesh.

Yet for all the ferociousness of the Chaos defence, they could no more hold back the ghostly legions through physical force than they could keep at bay a raging flood. Soon the enemy had encircled them, pressing in on all sides. Marauders were snatched into the air by too-long claws, tossed like rag dolls upon the tide of Death. Chaos Warriors were hacked down by dozens of spectral blades that pierced their heavy plate without leaving a mark. Slowly but surely, the defenders were driven from the walls, retreating into the central courtyard of Karheight. Nighthaunts wheeled and swooped about them, unleashing blood-chilling cries and delighting in the terror of their doomed prey. Just as the undead began to descend upon their quarry, the blaring of horns on the horizon drowned out their triumphant chorus.

SASKARID'S CHARGE

Lord Saskarid led the charge to Karheight at the head of his Deathsworn knights. The gates were closed and the entire fortress was shrouded in emerald light, so thick was the storm of Nighthaunts that surrounded it. There seemed no way for the Chaos Lord to reach his beleaguered warriors in the centre of Karheight. It was at that moment that the skies came alive with blinding rays of silver light. Like a great spear, the Silver Tower of the Tongueless Lord pierced the gloom, limned in the witchfire of the countless daemons that spilled from its ramparts and raced towards the undead. The Gaunt Summoner had unleashed the Unbound Flux, spreaders of insanity and destroyers of reason. Gibbering Heralds of Tzeentch capered and spun as they sent forth sorcerous flamebolts, each fiery missile exploding in a kaleidoscopic burst of madness that destroyed the minds of even long-dead spirits.

The ethereal and the daemonic smashed together like two mighty storm fronts, unleashing a boom of thunder that split open the earth and sent a shockwave rippling across the battlefield. As the Flux cavorted about, the Tongueless Lord himself swept down to do battle, his five most trusted Magisters riding upon Discs of Tzeentch at his side. Chainrasps and Revenants raced towards them and were swiftly incinerated in gouts of multicoloured flame. As one, the Tzeentchian wizards began to chant, working sparking arcane sigils into the air. The brimstone scent of sorcery burned away the stench of death, and the gates of Karheight shimmered as if glimpsed through a heat haze.

Lord Saskarid was only a few paces from the fortified gatehouse, his Karkadrak mount bounding relentlessly towards the seemingly impassable object, when the wizards' incantation reached its culmination. The targeted stretch of wall rippled and then melted into eldritch streams of boiling gold, smothering scores of Nighthaunts and opening a path for Saskarid and his cavalry charge. The Chaos Lord did not slow for a moment, the hooves of his mount hissing as they tramped over streams of sizzling metal towards the newly fashioned breach. He roared his praises to the Dark Gods as his Karkadrak leapt upon a lantern-bearing wraith, tearing the spectre to shreds with a great shake of its reptilian maw. Saskarid cleaved out left and right with his axe and cursed blade; wherever he struck, spirits burst apart in a spray of ectoplasm.

The Deathsworn barrelled in behind their master, lances levelled to run through dozens of helpless Nighthaunts. Inspired by the glorious spectacle of the seneschal of the Varanspire in battle, the defenders of Karheight renewed their efforts, hurling themselves upon their ghostly foes with abandon.

Even with the momentum of the battle shifted, the vast Nighthaunt host outnumbered the Chaos force many times over, and more were pouring through the breach with every passing moment. A whirling cyclone of gheists as massive as a Chamonic aetherstorm rose high into the sky, surrounding the Silver Tower of the Tongueless Lord and cutting off the daemonic reinforcements. The Eightpoints was bathed in an eerie witchlight that blotted out even the raging Chaos portal that encircled the crown of the Varanspire. From hundreds of miles around, the storm of Death could be seen flaring on the horizon.

Saskarid felt the power of the pantheon flow through him, filling him with hate and impossible strength. Atop his mount, he was a whirlwind of destruction, blasting a path through wave after wave of Chainrasps. The enemy sent their most hideous revenants against him – scythe-wielding Cairn Wraiths and macabre Knights of Shrouds – but none could lay a ghostly blade upon him, and all were hacked apart.

Even through the fug of his hatred, Saskarid knew that he could but delay the inevitable. Karheight would soon be overwhelmed, and all he could do was pray for a glorious death in battle. Steering his Karkadrak up the stairs of the perimeter wall and smashing a path through thickening clouds of undead, he emerged upon the ragged ramparts of the Dreadhold and looked out at the Shyish arcway. It was akin to looking upon a ruined dam, a ceaseless torrent of water bursting through its sundered cracks, except the swirling mass that forced its way through the shimmering Realmgate was composed entirely of incorporeal horrors. Saskarid hauled his mount about and turned away from the arcway. His gaze fell upon the Corpse Wastes, the vast expanse of jagged bluffs and open plains that stretched towards the Varanspire, now half-obscured by the dwindling light and chilling mists summoned by the dead. As he did so, a cruel smile played across his bloody lips.

They streamed towards Karheight in their thousands, drawn by the still-blazing sigil of the Everchosen that was the only light in the gathering darkness. The symbols burned into their skin or held aloft on banners of flayed flesh were wildly different: the eye of Nochseed, the horned skull of the Untamed Beasts, the devouring serpent of the Splintered Fang. Ironclad warriors of the Iron Golems charged alongside the skeletal, deformed sadists of the Unmade; hated foes who would, on any other day, delight in inflicting death upon one another were now united by the will of the Dark Gods to fight as a single, deadly force. The warbands of the Eightpoints had heeded the call.

It was the warriors of the Untamed Beasts who first reached Karheight. Screaming their praises to the Devourer of Existence, they hurled hooked harpoons into the mass of Nighthaunts. Ogor Breachers of the Iron Golems swung their weapon-limbs wildly as they barrelled through the fray. Graceful sword-artists of the Cypher Lords leapt and spun past their undead foes, always just out of reach as they cleaved with double-bladed swords. Raven-cloaked agents of the Corvus Cabal darted across the parapets, raining destruction from above. For the first time since the Endgate had burst open, the Nighthaunt assault began to falter.

Even as the warhordes of the Eightpoints rushed to face the onslaught of Death, they found themselves ambushed by shrieking hosts of Nighthaunts that came spilling out of the darkness.

THE VEILED LADY

The charge of Lord Saskarid had driven the Nighthaunts from the walls of Karheight and threatened to force the spectral host all the way back through the Shyish arcway. However, this was only a vanguard of the ghostly procession, and none other than the Mortarch of Grief herself would lead the next wave of incorporeal horrors.

An aura of freezing cold heralded her coming, sending crackling fingers of rimefrost creeping across the earth. This deathly chill brought with it a pall of utter hopelessness, a choking miasma of grief and loss that drained the will to fight from even the most heartless of killers.

As the charge of the Chaos reinforcements slowed, confronted with an overwhelming wave of sorrow, three spectral funerary carriages erupted from the Endgate. They trailed arcs of balefire as they smashed into the ranks of the Dark Gods' faithful. Bodies were swept up beneath the cursed vehicles' rattling wheels, and crackling forks of purple magic stretched out to blast the life from nearby foes. Saskarid's Deathsworn smashed a path towards the dread war machines, trying to drive lances through their cloaked coachmen, but they could not strike true. The strange etherealness of the ghostly carriages saw them flicker in and out of reality, and many of the knights' desperate thrusts struck nothing but empty air.

In the wake of the chariots' devastating assault, clouds of black rose petals floated down from the darkening sky, withering to curled husks before they ever touched the barren ground of the Eightpoints. As this funereal downpour continued, a mournful dirge drifted forth from the depths of the arcway, rising over even the clash and clangour of battle. Two skull-faced, spectral maidens glided through the portal; one was clutching a sealed blackwood casket, the other a shattered hourglass. Then came the woman in white – a spectre of death shrouded in alabaster robes, grave-rose vines winding like serpents about her skeletal body. As the handmaidens prostrated themselves before her macabre glory, Lady Olynder entered the Eightpoints. To look upon the veiled visage of the

Mortarch of Grief was to be stricken with purest desolation. In her frail frame was bound all the anguish of existence, and she wielded it like a scythe to strike her foes down. More than one warrior of the Dark Gods simply collapsed to their knees, exposing their throats to spectral blades rather than face such manifest despair.

Raising the Staff of Midnight high, the Mortarch of Grief let loose a keening wail, and bursting through the Endgate came the full force of Lady Olynder's retinue. Diamond-shaped formations of Hexwraiths galloped across the skies, blazing with evil balefire. Thousands of Chainrasps swept towards the Chaos forces, followed by whirling tempests of Spirit Hosts and scythe-limbed Harridans that shrieked in animalistic fury as they hacked and carved their prey apart. All that had come before had been merely a vanguard; this was the fell power of Dolorum unleashed in all its horror, and it shattered the will of Lord Saskarid's command. Outnumbered and lost in the grip of primal terror, hundreds of Marauders and entire warbands broke and ran, streaming through the breach in the fortress wall and fleeing across the open plain towards the distant Varanspire. The Tongueless Lord looked upon the slaughter as gheists swarmed over the retreating horde, bearing unfortunate souls to the ground and

tearing at their flesh with rusted blades. Summoning his remaining Magisters, the Gaunt Summoner soared back to the safety of his Silver Tower, daemons of the Unbound Flux swarming forward to cover his retreat. No sooner had he entered the summit of his great spire than the entire shimmering structure folded in upon itself, disappearing in a blinding burst of cerulean light and abandoning his allies to their fate.

Lord Saskarid saw the departure of his vizier and knew that the fortress was lost. Yet to flee now as the wretched sorcerer had done would be to incur the wrath of the Everchosen. The Chaos Lord had no intention of dishonouring himself in the eyes of the Dark Gods. He saw the veiled woman who led the army of the dead, and sheer fury banished the sorrow that had settled over him like a mantle. Kicking his mount into a charge, he barrelled through the advancing Nighthaunts towards the white lady, cleaving the spectral mounts from underneath Hexwraith riders with his infernal weapons. His Deathsworn knights thundered at his side, and no watching gods could doubt the bravery of their charge.

But they faced the Mortarch of Grief, no mere undead general but a master of war second only in authority to Nagash himself. Lady Olynder's veiled head turned as the Chaos Lord approached, and she stretched out a slender hand, curling her fleshless fingers like the contracting limbs of a dying spider. Saskarid felt his skin sloughing from his bones, turning to dust and ash even as his Karkadrak hurtled towards the Mortarch. Screaming with defiant rage, he raised his axe for a killing blow, hoping to strike the faceless horror's head from her body. Yet no more than a dozen paces from his quarry he heard his reptilian mount issue a gurgling death rasp beneath him. Succumbing to the flesh-withering curse, the beast stumbled and crashed to the ground. Saskarid was hurled into the air over its armoured head, striking the earth with bone-breaking force. When he finally came to his senses, Saskarid felt the icy touch of a pallid hand brush across his face and opened his eyes to see Lady Olynder staring down at him. The Mortarch of Grief slowly raised her veil, peeling back wisps of ghostly matter. Lord Namos Saskarid saw the true face of the Veiled Lady, and he knew a moment of pure terror before his heart burst in his chest.

THE PURSUIT

Darkness enveloped all. The supernatural pall brought forth by Lady Olynder spread out from the Endgate, smothering entire regions in its black embrace. Running, crawling, stumbling in terror across the plains, the routed armies of Karheight sought shelter – but there was none to be found anywhere in the Corpse Wastes. The Legion of Grief came on, an ethereal tide that engulfed their hapless prey; Chaos Knights were dragged from their coursers to be slashed to ribbons by knife-like fingers, while Marauders were dragged into the encroaching night. It was a massacre, and soon the lifeless bodies of thousands of slain warriors littered the earth.

Entire stretches of land that once echoed with the bestial howls of mutated predators and bloodthirsty killers were now eerily silent. As a deep and impenetrable night shrouded the land, fresh horrors crept from the mouth of the arcway. Some were no larger than a man, while the full immensity of others could only be imagined in the all-encompassing gloom. These were not creatures of ethereal matter; from a distance, one could hear the rhythmic tread of an army on the march and glimpse the glimmer of speartips in the darkness. A vast swathe of territory surrounding the Endgate had been claimed by the night. From the Nal-Ghoren Ridges as far south as the Forest of Eyes, Death held sway. Even the scrying crystals of the Tongueless Lord could not penetrate the veil

of darkness that the Nighthaunts brought with them. The Gaunt Summoner felt the first stirrings of fear. With Saskarid dead, it was he that would suffer the full wrath of the Everchosen when Archaon returned to see his domain marred by the presence of Death and another Realmgate torn from his grasp. Neither spirit-wraith nor ghostly queen could inspire terror in the Gaunt Summoner, but his own master was another matter. The Tongueless Lord knew that unless he pushed the Nighthaunts back through the arcway, he would suffer unimaginable torment at the hands of Archaon, who possessed his true name and, thus, the secret to unmaking him piece by piece. Not all was lost, however. Karheight had been a terrible defeat, but it was not yet a decisive one; the Gaunt Summoner still had many forces at his disposal, both mortal and daemonic.

So it was that the Tongueless Lord turned to his spymasters in the Cult of a Thousand Eyes. Agents of this Tzeentchian network were embedded in each murder-pit, reaver camp and slum-city in the Eightpoints, and as they heard their master's call, they wielded their influence to hasten the assembly of a fearsome Chaos host. Summons and threats were dispatched to each warlord and warlock that dwelt within sight of the Varanspire, demanding they make at once for Karheight. So too did the Tongueless Lord gather the entirety of his inner circle: Sorcerers, Daemon Princes and Magisters all, and amongst the most potent spellmasters in the Eightpoints. If sheer numbers could not turn back the Nighthaunt legions, then the Tongueless Lord would unleash an arcane inferno upon them that would obliterate even these cursed wraiths of the underworlds.

A TIDE OF SORCERY

The defeat at Karheight and the death of Lord Saskarid had left the Chaos defenders of the Eightpoints reeling. Yet here in this stronghold of the Dark Gods, they still outnumbered their foes many times over. Mortarch Katakros knew that he must press home the advantage decisively if victory was to be achieved.

In the face of relentless Nighthaunt assaults, the cohesion that had briefly united so many disparate Chaos warbands was shattered. The great mass of mortals divided into scattered pockets of resistance, which Lady Olynder began to encircle and obliterate one by one. The momentum of the Nighthaunt processions was formidable. The outer garrisons of the Varanspire loomed closer by the moment and, beyond that, the Citadel of Ruin itself – the grandest prize of all.

However, Death had not yet won the day. Archaon might have been absent from his throne, but the Eightpoints still boasted perhaps the mightiest armies in the realms. The Tongueless Lord's envoys had reached those great lords of Chaos who owed fealty to the Three-Eyed King, and many were now on the march towards the Corpse Wastes and the Endgate, sensing that an hour of great glory was at hand. Gradually, the immense war machine of Chaos lumbered into motion.

CHAOS RESURGENT

With Archaon's prime castellan slain, there was no single figure to unite the disbanded hordes. Instead, multiple Chaos Lords sensed an opportunity to fill the power vacuum and claim their own share of the glory. From the Famine Hills came the Darkoath Warqueen Marakarr Blood-Sky, back from her ill-fated foray into Shyish and with a vast horde of Marauders at her back – so large that when they took to the march, they blotted out the earth for miles around. Lord Crawen Caryx of Fell Keep led the Red Thousand, a host of Chaos Warriors wearing crimson plate, draped in salamander hides and armed with red-hot infernal blades and axes. These brutes marched beneath the fell glow of the Gorecradle, a smouldering Warshrine borne

aloft by mutant beasts. Meanwhile, Thlorg the Bilespewer emerged from the bubbling Flesh Marshes. The ancient Sorcerer rode upon a Manticore at the head of an enormous column of filth-smeared raiders and hulking, pus-bloated warriors in rotten green plate, the fly of Nurgle emblazoned upon their chests. These were warriors of the Blessed Sons, an infamous brotherhood that had spread the Plague Lord's word far across the Mortal Realms.

This mighty triumvirate made for the Shyish arcway, picking up stragglers from the disastrous sacking of Karheight along the way. Though not yet united as one, each force was a major threat in its own right. If these three armies were to converge upon the Shyish arcway before the Nighthaunts' gains could be consolidated, it would spell a premature end for Katakros' plans of conquest. The Mortarch's fleshless spy-birds observed the progress of the Chaos armies and relayed a stream of information back to their master. The lord of the Ossiarch Bonereapers knew that he must delay his foes – or risk disaster.

The Legion of Grief had driven the fleeing Chaos forces back as far as the Forest of Eyes when they encountered Marakarr Blood-Sky's army, the vanguard spilling from their lowland camps by the thousand. So followed some of the most horrific fighting of the entire campaign, the Nighthaunts and their mortal foes clashing in the shadowy copses of that cursed place. The Forest of Eyes was so named for the unblinking gaze of the souleater spiders that covered every surface and swarmed over every tree branch. These were no natural creatures. Infused with daemonic power and horrifically bloated, they fed not upon flesh but upon the souls of the slain.

Upon a carpet of skittering, shining bodies, Lady Olynder's pursuing army crashed into the great Marauder horde that the Warqueen had assembled. Those warriors that fell were instantly swallowed up by the tide; thousands of tiny arachnids swarmed into their ears, their nostrils, their screaming mouths. Their spirits were torn from their mortal frames and trapped upon the glittering webs that filled the forest. Neither were Chainrasp or Dreadscythe Harridan safe from such a fate, for these webs were spun from strands of unnatural sorcery and could ensnare the dead as easily as the living. Were these spirits capable of terror, they would surely have felt its touch as their incorporeal forms were stuck fast and a trillion crawling things advanced towards them out of the darkness.

Even as Lady Olynder was locked in this war of attrition, the Red Thousand hurled themselves into the fray. Lord Crawen Caryx himself charged at their fore, bellowing his praises to the god he knew as the Butcher King. The Red Thousand struck the Legion of Grief like a flaming fist, driving into the Nighthaunts' flank. As they slew, the symbol of ruin atop the Gorecradle blazed with unnatural fire, bathing the night in a bloody haze of crimson. As its Shrinemaster howled and ranted, spittle flying from his mouth, the Red Thousand wrought their fury upon the spectral dead.

Enraged at the stubbornness of a foe that refused to give in to hopelessness, Lady Olynder dispatched a flanking force of Hexwraiths led by Kurdoss Valentian, the Craven King, to drive the Red Thousand back. But even as these ghostly riders rose into the skies, seeking to strike from above into the heart of the Chaos Warriors' formation, they were set upon by thick clouds of buzzing flies. Thlorg the Bilespewer and a putrid flight of Plague Drones ploughed into Valentian's force from on high, the Sorcerer chortling behind his grated mask as he unleashed blasts of acidic bile that sprayed over the Hexwraith riders. Bilespewer had struck a pact with the Droning Guard of Septuklus, a legion of Nurgle daemons renowned for their mastery of the airborne attack, and the Plaguebearers' revolting fly creatures struck home viciously with envenomed stingers and bladed forelimbs.

Valentian took up his Sepulchral Sceptre and smashed pus-dripping fly-daemons out of the sky in a splatter of foul-smelling viscera. Though many called him the Craven King, the revenant lord was no meagre prospect in battle. Every blow of his accursed weapon sent another daemonic foe screaming back to the repulsive realm whence it had been summoned. Valentian and his foremost champions forced their way through the confusing tangle of limbs and membranous wings and plunged to earth, determined to fulfil their Lady's command. Yet as they broke through the clouds of flies, they saw below a horde of fresh Chaos troops seeping across the Corpse

Wastes; these warriors were pale and bloated, their flesh marked with the trilobed fly symbol of Nurgle. The Blessed Sons had arrived, and for once they fought not against their hated rivals, the crimson warriors of Crawen Caryx, but against the servants of Death who dared to intrude upon the dominion of the Dark Gods. Slamming the heavy mace head of his sceptre against his throne, the Craven King unleashed a breathless rattle of fury, the dust of ages spilling from his mouth. There was now no path to the crimson Chaos Lord who fought beneath the glare of the infernal Warshrine.

Slowly and at great cost, the Nighthaunts were driven from the Forest of Eyes back onto the open plain. It was there that their final defeat was decided. As if driven by some relentless predatory instinct, a tide of living magic swept towards the Forest of Eyes and struck the rear of Lady Olynder's procession. Gnashing jaws as tall as a gargant hissed and snapped at one another as they closed in on this new-found prey. Blazing skulls carved winding trails of flame across the ground, followed by a tide of displaced earth and rotting corpses. At the head of this arcane tsunami flew the Tongueless Lord. It had

taken every ounce of the Gaunt Summoner's power to corral this potent gathering of magic, but it soon proved its value. It swept through the Nighthaunt army in a surge of fire and devastation. For once, the ethereal nature of Lady Olynder's procession provided no defence at all.

From his vantage point above, Kurdoss Valentian observed the devastation grimly. He knew his Lady's wrath would be great, but he would not be smote by cursed blades nor suffer the lingering agony and humiliation as his shattered essence was slowly reformed. To the mocking laughter of his Wraith Heralds, the Craven King turned and fled the field; those Hexwraiths that had not been torn to shreds by flying daemon-things followed their liege-lord. Outnumbered and outmatched, the Nighthaunt charge was at an end.

With a scream of frustrated rage, Lady Olynder commanded her procession to fall back to the Shyish arcway. Yet even in defeat, her spectral legions had performed their task – their actions had delayed the armies of Chaos and left them entirely unprepared for the nightmare to come.

MARAKARR BLOOD-SKY

Across the Eightpoints, the name Marakarr Blood-Sky is spoken with fear and respect. A trusted member of Archaon's inner circle and a deadly warrior, the Darkoath Warqueen has united hundreds of tribes beneath her rule, taking the heads of any who would deny her authority. It is said that the Dark Gods have watched with delight as Blood-Sky wrought countless atrocities upon her enemies, and in return for her offers of sacrifice and tribute, the Warqueen has been granted visions and omens that lead her to victory after victory.

It was these god-granted visions that warned Marakarr Blood-Sky of the tremors that rippled out from Nagashizzar as Nagash worked macabre rituals in his attempt to create the Shyish Nadir. Gathering an immense Warhorde beneath her banners, Blood-Sky marched into the underworlds, intent on foiling the God of Undeath's plans. She might have triumphed, were it not for the interference of the Hammers of Sigmar. At the Battle of the Dustsprawl, a Lord-Ordinator of the first-forged Stormhost struck the

Darkoath Warqueen with a bolt of tempest magic, burying her and her champions beneath an avalanche of grave-soil.

When she awoke, Blood-Sky found that she had failed – the Shyish Nadir had been birthed by necromantic magic and her armies had been routed. But the Warqueen was not one to linger on what might have been. Taking up her axe and rune-marked shield, she embarked upon the long journey across the Ossian Dustsprawl, through the Realmgates of the Abyssal Fires and to the war-court of Archaon. Of that odyssey, there are but whispered rumours. It is said that when she finally arrived before the Three-eyed King, bloodied and smeared from head to toe in corpse-dust, Blood-Sky bared her neck and offered her life and soul in payment for her failure. Neither mercy nor forgiveness exist within Archaon's black heart, so none can tell why the Warqueen's life was spared. Yet survive she did, and ever since she has ruled over the Marauder hordes of the Eightpoints, awaiting the hour when she can exact her revenge upon Nagash and his servants.

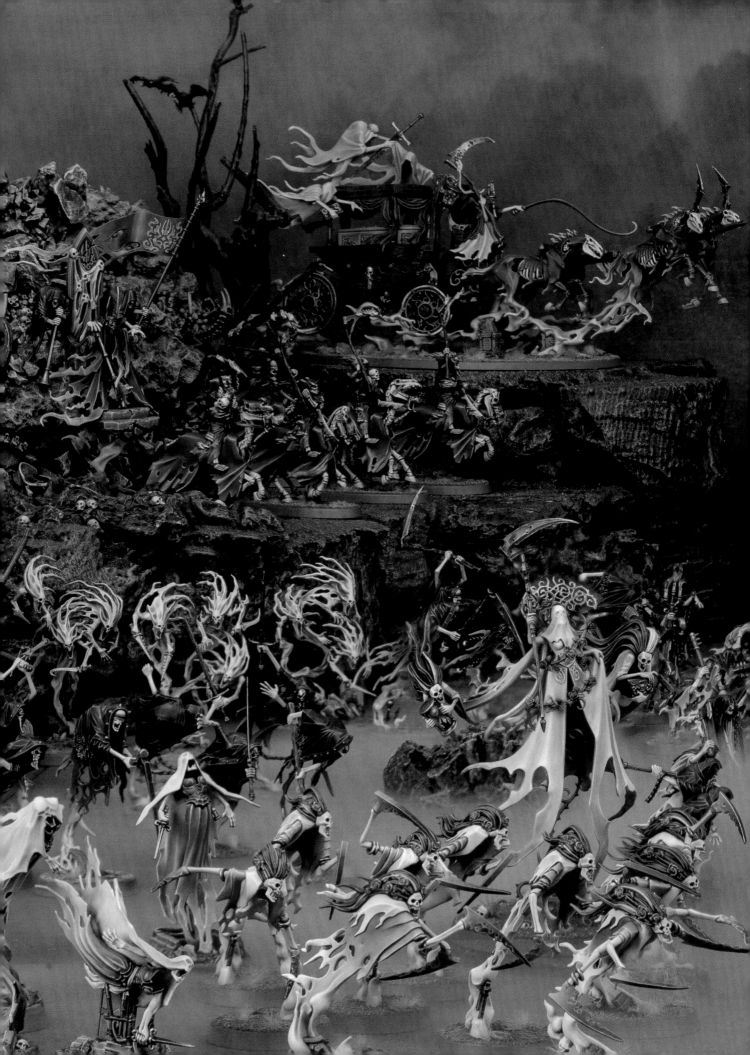

As Lady Olynder's Nighthaunts find themselves assailed on all fronts, the Gaunt Summoner known as the Tongueless Lord leads a furious assault by both daemonic and mortal hordes.

THE UNDEFEATED ONE

The Mortarch of the Necropolis entered the Eightpoints through the Endgate, alongside the largest host of Ossiarch Bonereapers ever assembled. While Lady Olynder's Nighthaunts were sweeping forwards in a shockwave of fear and panic, Katakros moved to consolidate the great gains that the deathly armies had made.

Borne aloft upon a necro-titan fashioned from the polished skeletons of slaughtered foes, Katakros the Undefeated entered the Eightpoints. He looked upon the ruination wrought by the Legion of Grief and was pleased; he had been right to trust in Lady Olynder's single-minded hatred of the living and the sheer unstoppable force of her spectral servants. Great progress had already been made, and now his Ossiarch Bonereapers would transform those gains into ultimate victory.

Marching through the Endgate in perfect order came the finest of his deathly legions. They included pristine warriors of the Mortis Praetorians, who had fought with Katakros since the earliest days of his ascension to the rank of Mortarch. Riding on the flanks were gleaming cavaliers of the Equumortoi, the feared Stalliarch Lords, on their soul-forged mounts. Katakros had even summoned liege-lords of the Crematorians and the Null Myriad to his grand crusade, along with their elite phalanxes. This was an army raised not only to lay siege to cities and townships but to lay waste to an empire and depose a self-proclaimed king.

Katakros knew the size of the task ahead of him. For all their wretched mortal weaknesses, the multitudinous hordes of Chaos that dwelt within the Eightpoints outnumbered even the mighty Ossiarch host many times over. This would be a war to challenge even his own peerless grasp of strategy and warcraft. Yet such paltry emotions as fear or nervousness were entirely alien to the Mortarch of the Necropolis. Even in life, he had been utterly assured when leading his armies to war. In death, he was content that he existed for but a single purpose – the total obliteration of the enemies of Nagashizzar.

THE BATTLE OF HARADH'S TORMENT

Katakros was determined to draw his foes to battle at a site of his choosing. He had dedicated his existence to the mastery of warfare and knew well that the advantage in any large-scale engagement always lay with the commander who dictated the terms of the battle. The blistering advance of Lady Olynder's Nighthaunts had granted him the leisure to choose his ground, and he had picked well. Haradh's Torment was a rocky mountain that rose from the Corpse Wastes to the north of the Varanspire, its razor-sharp peaks curled inwards like grasping fangs rising from the earth. Once it had been home to the fortress of Haradh the Breaker, a gargant warlord sworn to the Dark Gods who had dared to challenge Archaon the Everchosen's rule. Archaon had personally disembowelled the Breaker with the Slayer of Kings, leaving him to suffer a slow and painful death amidst the ruins of his ambition.

Thereafter, the mountain had been known as Haradh's Torment. With the banks of the acidic Black River on its right and an impassable chain of sharp-rocked cliffs to its left, it was in a highly strategic position. The great, fortified highway to the Endgate passed beneath the mountain's gaze, and so any reinforcements marching north to Karheight must pass within its zone of control. Though lines of ballista towers and direflame-spewing emplacements protected the highway, these had been among the first targets that Katakros and Lady Olynder had agreed upon before the initial assault through the Endgate. Those standing in the way of the Mortarch's plans had been cut off by the pall of darkness and swiftly overrun by packs of howling Bladegheist Revenants. The occupants were slaughtered messily and the weapons themselves shattered into splinters.

Even as this carnage was taking place, ranks of Mortek Guard spearmen were advancing up the arterial road, cutting down isolated formations of Chaos Warriors as they went. The iron core of Katakros' conquering armies, the Mortek Guard were soul-crafted soldiers possessed of splintered fragments of sentience. No mere skeletal automatons, they fought and moved with the skill of veteran warriors, responding instantly to the commands of their superiors but also interpreting those orders in the manner that seemed most ruthlessly efficient to them.

'Know this – any man or woman who fought at Haradh's Torment and survived will be blessed with the favour of the Ruinous Ones. Anyone who lived through that bloodbath is worthy of bearing a shield for me.'

- Darkoath Warqueen
Marakarr Blood-Sky

The highway leading from the Varanspire made its way upwards through a series of craggy bluffs and passed between the five peaks of Haradh's Torment. Its narrowest point lay at Impaler's Pass, where it carved through the largest of the mountainous edifices, a sheer drop to the gushing Black River on one side. It was here that Katakros planned to trap and destroy the three Chaos armies converging upon him. The highway here was still a league wide and had space enough for the Mortarch to deploy his elite cavalry, the dreaded Kavalos Deathriders. Yet it was also sufficiently narrow that enemies advancing towards his army would be forced into a bottleneck. The mountainous terrain beyond the road on the eastern side would be impassable to the majority of his mortal foes. Here, Katakros decreed, his force would hold and defeat an enemy three times their size.

The tripartite Chaos force had joined at last, united in an uneasy alliance by the Tongueless Lord. With the horde of Marakarr Blood-Sky racing ahead, this immense army made its way along the road towards the Shyish arcway. The long night still held sway, and only the flickering torches of thousands of Marauders and horsemen could be seen in the pitch-blackness. They charged into Impaler's Pass, which was narrow enough that it channelled the immense barbarian horde into a single, vast river of bodies.

It was then that the Darkoath Warqueen's host spied their enemy. Standing in tight formation at the far end of a gradually rising slope of scree and bone were thousands of Ossiarch warriors, silent and unmoving. Their shields were locked and readied, their nadirite spears glinting dully in the half-light. With roars of delight, the great mass of Blood-Sky's forces surged forwards, eager to crush their foes into dust.

Watching from the top of Impaler's Pass, on a shelf of rock that overlooked the mountainous valley, Katakros raised his hand and let it fall. From behind the ranks of the Ossiarch infantry, dozens of Mortek Crawlers crept into position. Artillery specialists known as war viziers plotted the trajectory of the onrushing horde and

unleashed their volleys of unnatural ammunition: great cauldrons of tormented soul-stuff that bathed the battlefield in ethereal light before smashing down amidst the surging mass of bodies. There, the cauldrons detonated in a screaming eruption of unholy energy, waves of madness and fear bursting forth and striking those nearby instantly dead.

Packed in so tightly together that they could not avoid the rain of missiles, many hundreds of Marauders were slain in that first charge. Nadirite spears thrust out and tore the life from their victims as the two lines met. Stabbing blades slit throats and opened bellies. Many Ossiarch Bonereapers fell in return, hacked to pieces by axes or clubbed to dust by flails, but the Mortarch of the Necropolis had chosen his terrain superbly. The slight rise of the scree slope gave the Mortek atop it a natural bracing point, while the increasing number of butchered Marauder corpses that littered the ground made it ever more treacherous for Blood-Sky's own warriors.

The Darkoath Warqueen herself led the attack upon the leftmost flank of the Ossiarch line, for that was the shortest route to the cursed siege weapons that were taking such a horrendous toll upon her horde. Lord Crawen Caryx and his Red Thousand joined her assault. The heavily armoured Chaos Warriors finally smashed a breach in the Mortek line. This was the kind of battle in which Caryx and his ilk excelled – when the lines of combat splintered into pockets of frenzied brutality. Their axes bit deep, hewing shields and splitting skulls. The sheer ferocity of this assault managed to throw back the disciplined defence of the spear-wielding undead, clearing a path to the Bonereapers' siege weapons.

On level ground at last, Blood-Sky and Caryx could see the lines of Mortek Crawlers ahead, still launching their deathly volleys. Chaos Warriors with twin axes hurled themselves at their foes, each wild swing of their weapons pulverising a leering skull-face into

dust or shattering a soultrap gem into a myriad darksome shards. In this brutal melee, the Red Thousand were in their element. Soon, Blood-Sky and Caryx had reached the line of Crawlers, where they set about butchering their skeletal attendants and smashing the winch pulleys and swinging arms of the siege weapons. Finally, the killing rain of necromantic energy was halted, and the forces of the Chaos triumvirate sensed their hour of victory was at hand.

From above, Thlorg the Bilespewer descended alongside his daemonic minions, while the heavy infantry of the Blessed Sons pushed along the very edge of the cliff that dropped to the gushing Black River below. Many times, skull-masked Necropolis Stalkers darted forward with ear-splitting shrieks, attempting to drive the rust-coated warriors of this elite band over the deadly precipice. But even their scything blades could not force the Blessed Sons back. Bleeding thick, viscous gore from dozens of wounds, the Blightkings ground on, methodically hacking their undead foes to splinters. Viewed from above, the shape of the battle began to deform, as the seemingly impenetrable front held by the Mortek Guard was eroded on both flanks.

Mortarch Katakros showed no outward sign of satisfaction, even as he saw the fighting progress exactly as he had anticipated. The enemy had taken the bait. Now was the time to enact his counter-strategy and seal their fate.

KATAKROS TRIUMPHANT

At last, Katakros the Undefeated had met his enemy in battle, forcing the enormous Chaos triumvirate to fight upon terrain he himself had chosen. The sheer size and ferocity of the enemy force seemed overwhelming, yet the Mortarch's foes had underestimated the strategic genius of the entity they now faced.

Only an Ossiarch warrior could have made the journey that Arch-Kavalos Zandtos and his Deathriders undertook. As Mortarch Katakros' armies were arranging themselves in defensive formation atop the slopes of Haradh's Torment, the Dark Lance of Ossia departed the crown of the mountain, winding his way through a series of deadly switchbacks and steep, treacherous cliffs to the banks of the Black River. In some places, the path was near vertical. Not even the most masterful mortal riders could have made such a descent, for their mounts would have stalled in terror or stumbled upon the loose fragments of bone and rock and tumbled into the gushing river below. Yet the soul-constructed steeds that Patru Zandtos and his retinue rode into battle placed not a single step astray, nor did they shy from the most lethal precipices. For this task, Zandtos had chosen the Stalliarch Lords, the most feared cavalry-lords amongst the ranks of the Ossiarch Bonereapers. Not a single rider out of many hundreds was lost on the long descent, and by the time the torches of the Chaos triumvirate were blazing along the rise to Haradh's Torment, the Arch-Kavalos and his armoured fist were already circling behind the enemy's position, concealed by the pall of night summoned by Lady Olynder and her Nighthaunts.

Just as the blunt force of Lord Crawen Caryx's Red Thousand and Marakarr Blood-Sky's great horde threatened to finally dislodge the Ossiarch Bonereapers from their position, a cry came up from the rear of the Chaos mass. The ground trembled as hundreds of nadirite-shod hooves thundered into the valley of Impaler's Pass. The worshippers of the Dark Gods looked on in mounting fear as two great arrowheads of heavy cavalry levelled their lances and charged. The Stalliarch riders were

resplendent in silver armour, their freshly fashioned mounts still slick-wet with gristle and gore. Arch-Kavalos Patru Zandtos himself rode at the tip of the spear. His glyphs of rank blazed bright green in the darkness as he smashed into a mob of tightly packed Chaos Marauders, his lance bursting through toughened leather and flesh in a messy splatter, his horned steed's grinding hooves crushing many more foes to paste.

As the tips of the wedge formations blasted open a path, the greater bulk of the riders widened the breach like a pathologist pulling apart the chest cavity of a corpse. Unable to fall back, pressed together too closely to form ranks and repel the ferocious charge, the warriors of Chaos were butchered by the score. Many were forced, screaming, over the edge of the precipice to splash into the flesh-melting currents of the Black River. Others were ground to a pulp against the cliffs of Haradh's Torment or simply suffocated amidst a stifling press of bodies. In a single, surgical strike, Zandtos had carved the triumvirate army in two. From his vantage point high above, Katakros watched in satisfaction, dictating observations and amendments to his battle theories to his Gnosis Scrollbearer.

From their hard-won position atop the rocky rise of the Pass, Marakarr Blood-Sky and her fellow generals could only spit and curse as they looked upon the devastation. The apparently faltering Mortek warriors to their front now swiftly reformed and came on anew, their numbers buttressed by shattered warriors refashioned into fighting shape by the incantations of Mortisan Boneshapers. Thlorg the Bilespewer was the first to fall. He met his end upon Zandtos' own lance, which thrust through his belly and sank deep into the back of the Sorcerer's Manticore, sending

mount and rider crashing to the ground. Bitter, black blood seeped from the gaping wound, and a groaning Bilespewer looked up to see the hooves of the Dark Lance's war-steed a split second before they caved in his skull.

'The Eightpoints, they call it. A land of rampant disorder, populated by the undisciplined and wretched masses of mortalkind. Would that I could snuff out the life from them all with a single strike of my war lance. I content myself with the knowledge that Lord Nagash's vision of purity shall triumph in the end; even these writhing, shrieking wilds will be silenced in the final reckoning.'

- Arch-Kavalos Zandtos, Dark Lance of Ossia

The Red Thousand, lost to battle madness beneath the glare of the Gorecradle, met the counter-charge gladly, and they bellowed their oaths of slaughter and ruin as the Ossiarch Bonereapers began to encircle them with nadirite spears. Marakarr Blood-Sky realised that it was useless to try and reach Lord Crawen Caryx, who was drenched in blood and bone-dust, carving apart all who strayed near him – be they comrade or foe – with mighty blows from his reaperblade. The hulking commander laughed madly as he slew, though his flesh and plate armour were riven with a hundred deep gashes.

All the while, the Tongueless Lord's magic sent whirling gouts of witchflame tearing through the Bonereapers' ranks. These sorcerous blasts transmuted many Mortek Guard into bubbling pools of molten metal, but try as he might, the Gaunt Summoner could not break his foe's seemingly impervious discipline. Mortisan Soulreapers sent icy bolts

of cursed soul-energy whipping towards the Tongueless Lord, and though his arcane barriers held out, they would not do so for long. With the enemy's cavalry running amok, the galling prospect of fleeing for a second time now seemed all but inevitable.

Though it filled her mouth with bile to admit it, Marakarr Blood-Sky also saw that the battle was lost. In fact, it would soon become a massacre – Caryx and his warriors were surrounded, while the flyblown forces of the Bilespewer were trapped against the cliffs overlooking the Black River and would soon be driven into its vitriolic embrace. The Blood God might smile upon such boundless slaughter, but the Three-Eyed King would not forgive the waste of valuable troops. Gathering her foremost tribal chieftains to her side, she sent their warriors crashing into the undead cavalry, trying to drive them from the mouth of Impaler's Pass and force open a route to freedom. Marauder Horsemen swept forwards, hurling axes and javelins at the Ossiarch riders in such volumes that the whirling missiles seemed like a downpour of steel rain. Many Kavalos Deathriders were

blasted from their steeds or dragged down by grasping barbarians to be hacked and torn apart. Blood-Sky's runic shield crushed skulls and shattered spears, and her axe hewed a path of ruination through her enemies.

Arch-Kavalos Zandtos had driven deep into the heart of the foe, and his lance and blade had claimed the lives of countless mortals. But he saw that the enemy was regrouping and that his Deathriders would soon be caught by the sheer mass of onrushing troops. Reluctantly calling a halt to the slaughter, he raised his spear and commanded his warriors to rally towards him. The two great wedge formations wheeled as one and fought free of the melee. The Ossiarch cavalry offered only the smallest of windows to their foes as they fell back in perfect order, but Marakarr Blood-Sky seized upon it. She drove her warriors onwards, forcing them through the small gap left by the retreating cavalry and out of the meat-grinder of Impaler's Pass. Only the last stand of the Red Thousand gave her the time and opportunity to make this desperate withdrawal; though they were not aware of it in their deranged

madness, the crimson-plated killers had fixed the attentions of Mortarch Katakros' legions. Their end was a bloody one indeed, glorious in its own macabre fashion. The Red Thousand destroyed many times its number that day, the tally of their kills forming a rampart of shattered bone about them. Yet, one by one, they fell to blades and bolts of soul-magic. Soon, only their master, Crawen Caryx, still stood, impaled a dozen times by nadirite spears and roaring his defiance at the dead. Mortarch Katakros gave an almost imperceptible nod of respect in recognition of the Chaos Lord's skill – and then ordered his Necropolis Stalkers forward to dismember him. With that final death, the battle of Haradh's Torment was over. Countless thousands of corpses littered the battlefield.

One would have expected Katakros to pursue his routed enemies, for his larger force surely would have caught the fleeing remnants of the Chaos triumvirate. Yet, to the astonishment of Blood-Sky, no such pursuit was forthcoming. Katakros the Undefeated had greater plans in mind – a strategy of conquest built upon the bones of his defeated foes.

THE ARX TERMINUS

Mortarch Katakros had won a magnificent victory, but his calculating mind observed that sheer momentum alone would not achieve his ultimate goals. As vast and powerful as they were, his legions were abroad in enemy territory. The Eightpoints was an immense continent, home to endless throngs of Chaos worshippers. In a conventional campaign of warfare on the open plain, even Katakros' mighty armies could not hope to triumph against such numbers. This was not even taking into account the warped and untrustworthy terrain or the predatory madness of the region's monstrous wildlife.

Even should he win another six victories as definitive as the defence of Haradh's Torment, it would not be enough to break the will of Archaon's hordes. Neither could Katakros afford to wait for a fresh cycle of bone-tithes to be delivered to the front lines in order to recoup his already significant losses. Thus, even before his legions had set foot in the Eightpoints, Katakros had identified the need for a strong, fortified position from which to launch further assaults.

This stronghold of bone and soul-matter would not only break any foes that sought to besiege it, it would also act as a supply post from which to reinforce his armies – not with the rations and equipment that a mortal army might require but with osseous matter stripped from the corpses of slain foes. With every enemy cut down and rendered into fresh materials, the Mortarch's own ranks would swell even as his opponent's forces dwindled.

Thus did the Mortarch of the Necropolis give the order to fall back to the Endgate. There, he began to finalise the construction of a dread citadel unlike any other. Gothizzar Harvesters lumbered to and fro, their skittering subsidiary arms scooping up torn remains, stripping the flesh with iron-hard fingers and then depositing the ivory remnants in the gory receptacles upon their ridged backs. Great caravans of the macabre devices trailed back towards the ruins of Karheight, which would become the foundation of Katakros' new fortress.

With the vast haul of bones and soul-stuff harvested from the battlefield of Haradh's Torment and Lady Olynder's many victories across the Corpse Wastes, Katakros' most revered Mortisan engineers were able to achieve remarkable results in a very short timeframe. Necro-thralls of the builder caste received these materials and, under the direction of their masters, began to construct Katakros' grand vision. These near-mindless labourers crawled across the surface of the fortress like maggots on a corpse, stitching together panels of weathered bone and hide, placing skull-lanterns enchanted with the flickering embers of rendered souls and fashioning murder-holes through which deathly missiles could be hurled. Soon, the black iron buttresses of the Chaos Dreadhold had been almost entirely reshaped or otherwise torn down, replaced with winding towers of bone and sinew that reached ever higher into the blackness of night like gigantic spinal columns.

Mortisan Boneshapers worked their intricate rituals, siphoning off the most potent ossified materials and sculpting them into vicious impaling hooks that would line the walls of the ever-expanding Ossiarch stronghold. Meanwhile, the Mortarch's favoured Soulmasons performed their own macabre arts, installing Mortek Crawlers, soulspear launchers and a variety of other hideously lethal war machines in key defensive positions along the bone walls.

Mortarch Katakros observed the ongoing works, adjusting the defences to the minutest detail, ordering spirit-hurling siege weapons to be deployed so as to cover the widest possible area and extending the perimeter walls so that they would funnel any besiegers into a series of murderous channels. In shape, the new fortress resembled a bony hand reaching out through the Endgate, each of its seven 'fingers' a formidably fortified wall in its own right, lined with traps and weapon emplacements. Katakros decreed that the remade fortress would be known as the Arx Terminus – the first citadel of Death to be raised in the Eightpoints.

Perhaps even mightier than the perimeter walls of the Arx Terminus were the vast chambers that lay below. These subterranean catacombs stretched deep beneath the earth. Home to workshops and soul-rendering chambers of the Mortisan caste, they also contained sepulchral cantonments and weapon foundries large enough to create thousands of fresh Ossiarch soldiers each day – provided that sufficient quantities of bone were supplied. Katakros had his nexus of resupply and reinforcement, but it would need to be fed with constant slaughter for it to function as he wished.

Within a matter of days, the grasping hand of the Arx Terminus rose high above the barren earth before the Endgate, each finger capped with a fortified obelisk that blazed with witchlight. Another, far larger tower rose from the centre of the structure – this was the Mortarch's Seat. From its summit, Katakros could oversee every facet of the Arx Terminus and conduct with precision any defence that might be required.

Though the deathly citadel was not yet functioning according to the Mortarch's exacting desires, it was still an all-but-unbreachable prospect for any besieging army – and Katakros was all too keen to test its lethal power on the hordes of the Eightpoints.

BESIEGED

The Mortarch of the Necropolis would not have to wait for long to see how the Arx Terminus functioned in a protracted siege. Already, more Chaos forces were converging on the Endgate and the Mortarch's newly completed citadel. The majority hailed from the Bloodbound Warhorde known as The Flayed. Deranged even by the standards of their Khorne-worshipping kin, these cannibals wore the bleached bones of those they butchered as armour, and many ritually flayed their own flesh before battle in a gruesome offering to the Blood God.

The Flayed were led by the Mighty Lord of Khorne Ghorun Thrax. This pale and silent giant spoke only when battle was joined, even then roaring naught but indecipherable threats and oaths in an ancient tongue. None but Khorne's daemonic servants could comprehend his rantings, but it nonetheless inspired a furious battle-frenzy in those who heard it.

The unruly Chaos host spilled over the horizon, a great tide of tattooed flesh and muscle. Standing astride the walls of the deathly citadel, the one they called the Undefeated examined the killing arcs of his Mortek Crawler arrays and was greatly pleased. Soon the enemy poured between the fingers of the Arx Terminus. Soul-reaper ballistae spat torrents of pure death magic from the walls, blasting scores of bestial creatures into dust and ash. Great chains of magically reinforced bone erupted from beneath the earth, corralling besieging warriors and rendering them easy targets for the necromantic artillery pieces above. Before long, the air was filled with eruptions of spirit energy and the screams of the dying.

There was little strategy to the assault beyond raw ferocity. Skull-capped siege towers forged from brass rumbled towards the walls, slamming into place before disgorging their living cargo. Thousands of battle-mad Bloodreavers and Blood Warriors poured out of the towers, only to meet the killing edge of a nadirite blade. Mortek defenders manning the walls methodically slew each scarred and blood-smeared figure that rushed at them, while teams of labour-thralls upended amphorae filled with tormented spirit-matter that turned those below into leathery corpses.

Three times did The Flayed push beyond the walls into the interior of the fortress. On one occasion, Ghorun Thrax himself led an assault that smashed open the gates of the Mortarch's Seat. There, he and his most fearsome Skullreapers were met by unbreakable formations of Immortis Guard, who carved the raging fiends apart with their glaives while scythe-wielding Mortisan priests reaped the spirits of the living.

After cleaving apart two Morghast Archai that sought to cut him down, Thrax was struck by a hail of necromantic energy from several Deathmages that withered the flesh on his right arm and one side of his face. Howling in agony and rage, the Lord of Khorne was driven from the tower and sent hurtling over the wall of the Arx Terminus. Even this was not enough to kill the blood-mad giant, but it put a temporary end to his rampages and robbed The Flayed of all cohesion. Degenerating into mindless savagery, they were smashed from the walls and either set to flight or methodically slain, their corpses used to stitch together any breaches in the walls of the deathly fortress. Soon, even the most severe damage inflicted by warriors of The Flayed had been repaired.

The other worshippers of Chaos amongst the vast throng fared little better. The splayed-hand design of the Arx Terminus was such that the arcane weapons mounted upon each outstretched wall could cover the next, creating an all-encompassing web of fire and necromantic magic that the besiegers were forced to endure before they even reached the fortifications. Thousands were slain in a matter of hours as the Siege of the Arx Terminus escalated. Their lifeless bodies formed a rampart for their fellows, but it was simple enough for the Mortisan priests to work their necromantic spells upon the corpse piles, commanding them to ensnare and tear apart those who set foot upon them.

Chaos Gargants tore and smashed at the walls, hammering their fists against bone until it splintered beneath their onslaught. Yet the Arx Terminus was designed to withstand such punishment; even as sections of wall were sundered, Boneshapers and Soulmasons wove spells of remaking that knitted together fractures and closed breaches. And all the while, the scores of Mortek Crawlers that lined the walls spat their torrents of cursed spirit-stuff down upon the besiegers, filling the skies with a deadly rain of glowing balefire that unleashed madness and terror wherever it fell.

There was no way past the deadly interlocking defences of the Arx Terminus. Mortarch Katakros observed the slaughter from atop the citadel's great tower and was highly satisfied. His calculations had been exactly perfect, as always. The enemy had been pinned and torn apart, just as planned. The tattered remnants of The Flayed were soon fleeing from the shadow of the Arx Terminus, leaving their dead behind as yet more fodder for the Ossiarch legions.

Thus did the Mortarch's enemies break upon the walls of the Arx Terminus and, in so doing, provide their victorious foes with the final materiel required to complete the construction of Katakros' great citadel of Death.

The Battle of the Arx Terminus was a bloodbath of the most terrible kind, as slavering hordes of Chaos-worshippers hurled themselves against the deathly fortifications of Katakros' fortress.

MORTARCH KATAKROS

Katakros strides the Mortal Realms as a colossus of war. Accompanied by his royal legions, this immortal strategist coordinates not just the battle before him but also a sprawling campaign across the lands. Those who seek to slay him are either dispatched by his champions or cut down by the glaive of the Mortarch himself.

Orpheon Katakros is the emperor of an undying elite, and he goes to war with all the pomp and circumstance that befits his station. Distrustful of steeds ever since the disastrous chariot charge that cost him his life, he simply strides to battle with the surety of a god. It is his wont to take a commanding vantage point from which he can look down on the battlefield, just as he did in life, surrounded by his most valued aides – though, like their master, they too are long dead.

The regiments of the Katakrosian army are the Mortarch's blade and shield, for he has no wish to sully himself with the business of violence. Instead, he focuses on more cerebral matters, his indomitable will reaching out to invigorate and inspire his troops whenever his gaze passes across them. A Katakrosian legion is a perfectly honed tool of war, a military body of surpassing discipline guided by the genius of a leader steeped in centuries of experience. His time spent trapped within the Stormvault near Lake Lethis did not still his mind; having dwelt on matters of revenge across the entirety of the Age of Chaos, it is now a more sophisticated and dangerous weapon than ever before.

The supernatural focus that Katakros brings to the art of war is facilitated by his entourage. At his right hand is his Liege-Immortis, the high-helmed champion who commands the Immortis Guard that protect him on the field of battle. At his left is his Prime Necrophoros, the bearer of Katakros' sacred banner. All creatures – living or dead – that can see the glinting black capstone of his standard raised upon the horizon will hear the Mortarch's stentorian tones loud and clear in their minds whenever he speaks.

Often, Katakros will wage several wars at once. Using the bird-like messengers of his Aviarch Spymaster, he coordinates overlapping campaigns that stretch across thousands of leagues. Even as he breaks the foe's army piece by piece, he dictates documents for their surrender to his keepers of knowledge, the Gnosis Scrollbearers – for should enough of the enemy survive to provide a profitable source of tithe, he will seal their fate by binding them in inescapable arcane contracts.

In Nagash's eyes, Katakros is the perfect general. He was remade in the idealised form of an exemplar of undeath – a fact he knows full well, which further compounds his monstrous sense of superiority. Should a supplicant grovel enough or prove to be particularly silver-tongued, the Mortarch of the Necropolis can be bargained with. He will just as willingly subjugate nations through his own twisted form of diplomacy in order to secure a vassal state – and thereby a steady supply of bone – as he will crush them through military action. To him, it is one and the same. Either way, he will have his victory in the end.

THE MORTIS PRAETORIANS

The majority of the Ossiarch contingents dispatched by the Mortarch to lay siege to the Eightpoints hailed from the Mortis Praetorians, the chosen guard of Katakros himself.

Since the Age of Myth, the Mortis Praetorians' ability to wage war with uncanny speed and efficiency has won them countless battles. The philosophy of Orpheon Katakros is embedded in every one of his prized legions, a bone-deep impression of his martial values that forms an intrinsic part of their composite souls. These core principles are bolstered and shaped by the personalities of his favoured generals. Such was the Mortarch's need for conquest that he ripped the souls of the generals who had served him well in life from their mausoleums and gave them to his Mortisans, who painstakingly split them through a harrowing process called spiritual distillation. In doing so, he could instil a tiny part of each of these officers into each favoured cohort.

Owing to the unique nature of their construction, the total number of the Mortis Praetorians remains a constant. They are known to the other Ossiarchs as the Ten Thousand Cohorts – never fewer, never more. The Chaos defenders of the Eightpoints swiftly learnt to hate the green-and-ivory armoured warriors of the Katakroi above all others, for they fought with breathtaking skill and formidable relentlessness.

RELENTLESS CONQUEST

With a stronghold constructed within the territory of his foes, Mortarch Katakros and his ally Lady Olynder began a campaign of brutal conquest. Uniting their vastly powerful legions as one, they swept towards the mighty fortress of the Varanspire, crushing all in their path.

Katakros' assault upon the Eightpoints began to gather fearsome momentum. With the highways cleared all the way to the Citadel of Ruin and the most pressing of his enemies routed, the Mortarch of the Necropolis advanced with all haste towards the seat of power. Desperately, the Tongueless Lord hurled horde after horde at the oncoming Ossiarchs, but each was crushed in turn, and the relentless march continued.

His offensive did not go uncontested. At the Gate of Flayed Hearts, the Mortarch found himself assailed by thousands of purple-skinned beastmen and hulking Bullgors who emerged from twisted copses to attack the flanks of his columns. It was Katakros himself who dispatched the one-eyed Bray-Shaman that led this ambush, disembowelling the impudent creature with an artful slash of his blade Inda-Khaat. At the Bridge of Molten Screams, his Necropolis Stalkers and a retinue of his elite Immortis Guard fought for more than a day to find a way through the ferocious defence upheld by the Carrion Hounds' chosen shields. All the way, mounted Marauders struck at the columns of marching undead. While each brief attack delayed the Mortarch's progress, the aggressors were swiftly driven off either by Zandtos and his Stalliarch Lords or by the Mortek warriors' spears.

The butchery was cold and methodical. Katakros left nothing alive in his wake – everything, from the screeching Raptoryx that fled before his advancing legions to mighty Chaos Lords and mutated beasts of the wild, was remorselessly slaughtered. Totems and pillars of worship were smashed asunder, forests burned and fleeing foes scythed down by Deathriders. 'Leave nought but ash and silence,' the Mortarch of the Necropolis had decreed, and his warriors fulfilled

his order with merciless precision. Wherever the Ossiarchs roamed, the anarchic wilderness of the Eightpoints was transformed into a sterile wasteland.

There was simply no general to be found amongst the Chaos hordes that matched the genius of Mortarch Katakros. Every obstacle thrown into his path was solved through a combination of tactical brilliance and ruthless momentum. Spurning conventional wisdom, the Mortarch sub-divided his forces into smaller cohorts as they progressed. Whenever such a detachment encountered a sizeable enemy force, they would form squares and give battle while the Emissarian caste dispatched urgent messages to nearby forces. The enemy would be drawn in by an apparent opportunity for victory against an outnumbered foe – only for Ossiarch reinforcements to swiftly appear upon the horizon.

The secret to this strategy lay in the fortifications Katakros had so painstakingly laid down in front of the Endgate. The necro-factories of the Arx Terminus devoured shipment after shipment of bone taken in the aftermath of Olynder and Katakros' victories. Marching up from the catacombs of the great citadel came a continuous stream of Mortek reinforcements. The greater the victories achieved by the Mortarch of the Necropolis,

the more swiftly his armies were swollen by these additional soldiers. Time and again, Katakros' foes were utterly unprepared for the swiftness with which his armies regrouped, reformed and struck anew.

Racing ahead of the Ossiarch cohorts were Lady Olynder's Nighthaunts. The battle at the Forest of Eyes had depleted the Legion of Grief greatly, but the aura of death and horror that swirled about the Arx Terminus provided fine fodder for the Veiled Lady. She summoned forth fresh hosts of Chainrasps and other spectral killers from the underworlds and, under a pall of choking sorrow, resumed her war against the living with greater intensity than before.

TO THE GATES OF THE VARANSPIRE

Inexorably, the two Mortarchs pressed closer and closer to the monolithic Varanspire. They passed the armoured bridge-forts on the border of the Corpse Wastes and continued into the industrial hellscapes beyond. Here, gargantuan forge-bellows spat sulphur and ash high into the air, and masses of withered and tormented slaves toiled their agonising lives away to fashion the blades and armour for Archaon's endless legions. The blackened, skeletal outlines of nightmarish factories stretched into the distance as far as the eye could see. Immense chitinous behemoths thrust spiked proboscises deep into the earth, eagerly lapping up the cursed metals that flowed far beneath the crust of the Eightpoints.

This blighted region of heavy industry was known as Angazkul-Grend, meaning Ironskull Forgesprawl in the tongue of the duardin slavemasters who stoked its infernal flames. It was no accident that Katakros had brought his armies here; should

Angazkul-Grend be pillaged and burned, it would rob Archaon and his armies of a potent source of weapons and war machines, for many daemonic engines were forged in its smoking furnaces.

The assault began with typical precision and efficiency. Scores of Mortek Crawlers embarked on a thorough bombardment of the industrial sprawl. Instead of flames and smoke, each emerald missile unleashed a swirling cloud of tormented spirit-stuff. So intense was the barrage that soon vast areas of Angazkul-Grend were swallowed up by raging spirit-storms that spread like wildfire. Screams of maddened terror could be heard for leagues around. When the Crawlers finally ceased their volleys, the Mortek Guard advanced into the tangled, metal jungle, spears and nadirite swords at the ready. They were met by a fierce resistance. Not only did the duardin slavemasters unleash their daemonic siege-cannons and other deranged creations against the advancing Ossiarchs, but the labyrinthine alleys and smoke-spewing workhouses provided the perfect killing ground for ambushing packs of Chaos Warriors. The sadistic reavers known as the Unmade had claimed an entire district of Angazkul-Grend as their own, decorating it with the flayed corpses of their victims – and, in some cases, the skinless, mewling bodies of those they had yet to offer the mercy of oblivion. They launched constant raids upon the undead interlopers, bounding from the shadows to rip and tear at their prey before disappearing as swiftly as they had appeared. Such defiance was spirited, but it soon faltered and broke. Every living thing that the Ossiarchs found, whether thrall, warrior or otherwise, they dragged out into the open and slew, leaving the piled bodies for their Harvester engines. Inch by inch, Angazkul-Grend was purged of enemies, contested structures cleared out with volleys of cursed steles inscribed with soul-shredding revenge curses. It was not long before the disciplined squares of the Mortek Guard had reached the far side of the forge-sprawl and emerged upon the banks of the Soulsplinter River – an enormous, winding tributary filled not with clear water but with screaming, burning souls.

Beyond, Katakros could see the rising outer fortresses of the Citadel of Ruin, home to the Empty Throne. The Mortarch of the Necropolis clasped his hands in triumph, but the shrieking cries of his carrion messenger birds drew his eyes to the east. There, fire wreathed the horizon. Katakros felt the ground tremble beneath him.

ARCHAON'S WRATH

Mortarch Katakros had devastated vast regions of the Eightpoints and driven his foes before him wherever his armies marched. Yet as the skies above the Varanspire boiled and the earth trembled to the sound of sulphurous hoofbeats, the Undefeated knew that the real battle had only just begun…

The land itself recoiled at his coming. Mountain ranges erupted in torrents of boiling blood. Savage plains writhed and shivered, each blade of razorgrass instantly transformed into a hissing, three-headed serpent. Clouds of crimson, violet and viridescent flame screamed across the skies, and the foulest abominations crawled from their lairs, howling in terrible anticipation. Lakes boiled. Forests burned. The Dark Gods roared in triumph.

Descending towards the Ossiarch Bonereapers came a black host, resplendent in the ruinous panoply of Chaos. They were joined by daemonic forms that boiled from the skies in untold numbers; great bat-winged Bloodthirsters surged towards Katakros and his Bonereapers alongside blade-finned Screamers of Tzeentch and grotesque flocks of filth-dripping Plague Drones. Scintillatingly beautiful and androgynous forms laughed in exultation as they drove bladed chariots across the barren earth in search of fresh souls to torment. This was the Legion of Chaos Ascendant – a force of purest desolation unleashed only on those rare occasions when the Ruinous Powers made common cause. At the fore of this infernal host rode a towering figure with a flaming sword, mounted atop a three-headed chimeric monster with wings as wide as a fortress gate. Archaon the Everchosen had returned to the Eightpoints, and he brought with him the wrath of the Dark Gods. All ancient hatreds had been put aside as the Ruinous Powers sought to expel the armies of the pretender-god Nagash from their rightful domain.

Acting with formidable speed, Katakros immediately dispatched a volley of orders. With an efficiency that would have been impossible for any mortal army, the immense

shield of the Ossiarch formations wheeled about to meet this new enemy. They formed a line along the banks of the Soulsplinter River, with the ruins of Angazkul-Grend at their back. Patru Zandtos ordered his Kavalos Deathriders into formation, and hulking Morghast Archai moved to the head of the battle line. Despite himself, the Mortarch of the Necropolis felt a shiver of anticipation ripple through his lifeless form. This was the battle he had been fashioned for, a test beyond anything that he had yet faced. If his death mask of a face had been capable of forming the expression, Katakros would have smiled broadly.

For his part, Archaon knew only a volcanic fury as he looked upon the creatures that had dared trespass into his domain, forcing him to abandon his quest to free Slaanesh. By now, the aelven gods would surely have restored the wards that concealed their prisoner and transported the chained god to some other hidden corner of Uhl-Gysh. Archaon's hand gripped the hilt of the Slayer of Kings hard enough to draw blood. He drove his heels into Dorghar's flank, urging the Steed of the Apocalypse towards the skeletal shieldwall. Eager drool spilled from Dorghar's Bloodthirster head, while the one that bore the grotesque visage of a Great Unclean One chortled wetly at the carnage to come.

The Varanguard drove their own daemonic steeds on in the wake of their master. The Eight Circles

of this ruinous order had sent their mightiest killers to scour the Eightpoints clean; these were the Knights of the Empty Throne, heralds of the Everchosen, and their fury spelled the doom of nations. Each warrior amongst the dread champions of Archaon was determined that no undead wretch would be left standing when the slaughter was done. Even the dead would be made to suffer eternally for their arrogance and hubris.

Mortek Crawlers spat streams of witchfire into the sky, limning the clouds with emerald light. The ethereal missiles arced and fell into the mass of advancing bodies, blasting armoured riders from their mounts. It barely slowed the charge. At the command of his liege-lord, Arch-Kavalos Zandtos led his Deathriders forward in their thus-far-impenetrable wedge formations. The finest cavalry in the armies of Nagash were keen to test their lances against the famed Varanguard, and none more so than the Dark Lance of Ossia. The ground shook as the two forces converged, coming together in a thunderous clash of nadirite and cursed steel. Armour crumpled and bone shattered. Kavalos riders were sent hurtling through the air, smashed to pieces by the heavier daemonic steeds of the Varanguard. In turn, Zandtos and his champions thrust their lances through grilled helms and into warped and twisted faces marked with the vile corruptions of the Dark Gods. This time, the Kavalos Deathriders could not shatter their foes with the force of their momentum; the Varanguard repelled their every desperate charge.

Archaon himself sent Dorghar straight into the heart of the Deathrider formation. The Steed of the Apocalypse lashed out with hooves and whip-like tails, shattering skull-helms and spears. His three daemonic heads ate their fill of ossified armour and cursed soul-stuff, snapping out to devour Kavalos Deathriders whole or to tear the heads from their steeds. And all the while, the Slayer of Kings wove a pattern of death through the fray. Zandtos fell there, on the banks of the Soulsplinter, knocked from his mount by Dorghar's swiping tail, his chest crushed to splinters. Loyal retainers retrieved the soultrap gem, weapons and marks of office that belonged to the Arch-Kavalos; the Dark Lance of Ossia would be remade anew, though his mighty Stalliarch Lords had been battered aside by the mailed fist of the Varanguard. It was a sore blow, but Katakros had expected it – Zandtos had bought time for the Mortarch to fully deploy his army.

Even now, Lady Olynder's legion was sweeping above the ruins of Angazkul-Grend, screaming towards the flank of the Everchosen's host. Yet before they could reach their intended prey, the onrushing gheists were engulfed by snaking bolts of shadow magic. Bursting from the black clouds came the bat-winged form of Be'lakor, the Dark Master, and with him the Legion of the First Prince, formed of the daemonic footsoldiers of Khorne, Tzeentch, Nurgle and Slaanesh. Such a wild gathering could only be controlled by one as fearsome as Be'lakor, who – it was said – had claimed the favour of all four Dark Gods long before Archaon had done so. His immense force fell upon the Nighthaunts as a crashing wave, and their cursed blades and unnatural magic proved far more lethal against beings of ethereal matter than had the swords and axes of mortal warriors. With their allies locked in brutal combat, the Ossiarchs' position suddenly seemed far more precarious. Archaon the Everchosen had called upon all of his subjects to purge the Eightpoints of Katakros and his Bonereapers once and for all. Warhosts of Slaanesh smashed into the spear-ranks of the Mortek line, driving their bladed chariots deep into the soul-constructs' formation. They howled and shivered with delight as they lashed out at their victims, revelling in every gouge and stab

wound inflicted upon their bodies in return. The normally fractious Hedonites of Slaanesh put aside all differences as they exulted in the slaughter – conquering Invaders of the Lurid Haze battled alongside the Pretenders of the Faultless Blades and the Godseekers of the Scarlet Cavalcade, who had been swept along in the wake of the Everchosen's quest to free the Dark Prince. Surrounded by a miasma of sickly incense, the disparate worshippers of Slaanesh eagerly indulged their passion for violence. Yet as deadly as their writhing dance of blades was, they could not breach the tightly packed squares of the Ossiarch Bonereapers.

Wading through the Soulsplinter River came Plaguebearers of the Munificent Wanderers, led by the notoriously generous Great Unclean One known as Thrombolhox the Giving. These repulsive warriors were eager to share their suppurative gifts with the strange osseous constructs. Katakros' elite Mortis Praetorians met them on the bank of the river, and the shore was soon clogged with rotten blood and fragments of splintered bone. The battle seemed evenly matched, but soon the Ossiarchs caught sight of filth-stained sails upon the horizon. Great plague-hulks drifted down the Soulsplinter River, bearing the corroded trident of the Drowned Men. These were the followers of the mighty Gutrot Spume, one of Nurgle's most favoured mortal champions. Lumbering from the rotting hulls of their ships, bloated Blightkings charged into battle, their verdigrised armour seeping coppery grime that stained the earth in their wake.

Despite the relentless onslaught, Katakros' flanks held strong, and his Mortek Crawlers continued to spit death at the foe. So long as the Ossiarchs gave no ground, they could grind their foes down. The Mortarch ordered his Morghast troops forward to support Lady Olynder, and the majestic, ornately armoured sentinels took to the skies, skinless wings beating furiously as they rose over the carnage of the front lines. Before

they could descend upon the daemon tide assailing the Veiled Lady, however, they were struck by a storm of blazing red comets. Encased in armour of midnight black, four Bloodthirsters of the Baleful Lords set upon their prey, axes and whips opening gaping wounds in osseous armour and sending several Morghast Archai tumbling from the sky. In response, Morghast Harbingers leapt upon the backs of the greater daemons, hacking and stabbing with swords that passed through armour and flesh to rend the essence beneath.

Even as he watched the enemy gather on all sides, Mortarch Katakros knew no trepidation. It had only been a matter of time until the full panoply of the Dark Gods was unleashed against him. All had been foreseen and accounted for.

THE DARK MASTER

Be'lakor is the First Prince of Chaos, a being of pure darkness who has haunted the realms for time immemorial. Amongst the Daemon Princes, he alone has gained the favour of all four Dark Gods. This makes him an enemy to be greatly feared, for he can call upon almost limitless numbers of daemonic footsoldiers. Known as the Legion of the First Prince, Be'lakor's nightmarish army has destroyed empires and kingdoms beyond number over aeons of slaughter, aided at all times by the cunning manipulations of its master.

None but the Dark Gods know Be'lakor's true origins, but his antipathy with Archaon is legendary and surely stems from the Three-Eyed King's own status as the Everchosen – an epithet that the First Prince might rightly claim himself. Nevertheless, the two have joined forces several times to conquer and despoil, always with formidable and terrible results.

UNSTOPPABLE HATRED

Whatever order the Mortarch of the Necropolis had sought to impose upon the Battle of the Varanspire was sundered by the untrammelled ferocity of the Chaos assault. His Ossiarch legions fought with unflinching skill; even the lowliest warriors slew many times their number before being smashed to dust by the axe of a raging Bloodthirster or immolated by the scintillating wyrdflame of the Unbound Flux. Viewed from above, the Ossiarch Bonereapers formed an island of black and bleached bone amidst a roiling sea of many-coloured forms, its borders slowly eroded by the ceaseless onslaught.

Mortarch Katakros ordered all of his Gothizzar Harvesters into the assault. The towering death engines plunged into the midst of the daemonic horde, their scythed fists pulping bodies and smashing skulls to pieces even as the murderous juggernauts trampled dozens underfoot. Kept unnaturally sharp by Shyishan magic, the Harvesters' blade-limbs could hew through even the thickest daemonic hide – the Great Unclean One known as Grolthlurrp the Merry was set upon by half a dozen of the constructs, which carved open his great belly and pulled out his rancid innards with their subsidiary limbs.

Despite their formidable stand, the Ossiarchs were simply outmatched by the full might of the Ruinous Powers. The Legion of Chaos Ascendant was a spiked gauntlet that drove its way through the Ossiarchs' seemingly impenetrable shieldwall. Bloodletters overran the disciplined defence of the Mortek Guard, bounding over shields into the midst of their prey, swiping their brazen blades to shatter the bone-forged warriors into fragments. Pink Horrors spewed unnatural flames, and – standing as giants amongst the flood of lesser entities – the greater daemons of the Chaos Gods unleashed their full and terrible power upon Katakros' army. To the warbands and reaver hordes of the Eightpoints, the apocalyptic slaughter was akin to a vision of glory sent by their malign deities.

Once more, the denizens of the Eightpoints surged from their lairs, sensing blood in the water. Iron Golems, Unmade, Splintered Fang and Untamed Beasts fought alongside the infernal creatures that they worshipped as gods, lost in the throes of ecstasy as they took their revenge for the horrific losses at Karheight and at the massacre of Haradh's Torment.

The Mortek line wavered under this onslaught. Hekatos officers reshaped their lines with consummate skill, ushering fresh spearmen to fill the ragged gaps in their formations, but it was like trying to plug the holes in a broken dam. For every daemon impaled or mortal reaver cut down by a nadirite blade, ten more surged forward to take their place.

Even worse, at that critical moment, Be'lakor the Dark Master struck a fateful blow against Lady Olynder, driving the Blade of Shadows through her veiled form. The Mortarch of Grief unleashed a death-scream that rose above the clangour of battle and stole the life from many who heard it. Even Be'lakor's ensorcelled sword could not end the curse of Lady Olynder once and for all, but with that fatal strike, her essence was banished from the Eightpoints. Without the Veiled Lady's macabre presence to unite them, the Nighthaunts were swiftly overcome by the ferocity of the Legion of the First Prince. Katakros' allies were swept from the field. His Ossiarchs now fought alone. Recognising that the final hour was at hand, with a regal gesture, Mortarch Katakros

sent forth his reserve formations, including the Scions Praetoris – the most trusted champions amongst his elite Immortis Guard. Each of these towering constructs was created from the souls of warriors who had fought with him for centuries beyond counting. The Scions' battle shields were as lethal as their halberds. In methodical and rhythmic combinations, they drove their foes backwards then lashed out with their polearms to strike a killing blow. Though they added to their glorious legacy of deeds in the twilight moments of the battle, even their grim charge could not avert the inevitable.

As Dorghar circled the battlefield on high, Archaon the Everchosen laid eyes upon the being who had dared lead this intrusion into his rightful domain. Mortarch Katakros did not fight at the forefront of his armies like Archaon himself; instead, he observed the carnage from a ridge of razor-sharp rocks overlooking the banks of the Soulsplinter River. Phalanxes of Immortis Guard stood sentinel over their master, and a twenty-strong retinue of Morghast Archai formed a shield of ossified armour around him.

Boiling, animal fury coursed through Archaon's veins as he met the skeletal lord's gaze. The simmering rage of the Three-Eyed King caused hot blood to pour from the skies, and the Soulsplinter burst its banks in a flood of molten soul-stuff, drowning undead and daemonic beings alike in its cursed waters.

Archaon kicked his heels into Dorghar's flank and the Steed of the Apocalypse blazed like a comet towards the Ossiarch general. Volleys of cursed spirits arced towards the descending behemoth, but Dorghar's monstrous heads simply devoured the deadly missiles, the necromantic magic dissolving in the heat of the Everchosen's rage. As the Three-Eyed King barrelled towards him, Katakros raised Inda-Khaat and took up the Shield Immortis. This battle would end with a duel between two titans of war.

The tyrant of the Eightpoints advanced, his blazing eyes fixed upon Katakros, the sheer force of his hatred turning the air to a sweltering haze.

Katakros only watched, impassive, as his army collapsed around him. The daemon tide had broken the Mortek shieldwall and riotous, howling shapes swept across his lines, slaughtering as they went. As the Everchosen pressed closer, he dictated some final observations to his Gnosis Scrollbearer.

'Palisade of blades ineffective against daemonic attacks,' he said. 'Concentration of Crawler bombardments far more effectual.'

Archaon was only twenty paces away now, the ranks of Katakros' personal guard little more than a smouldering ruin of charred bones.

The Mortarch gestured forwards with Inda-Khaat, and his attendants drew their weapons and advanced towards the foe. His Prime Necrophoros, bearing aloft the Mortarch's personal banner, managed to gouge a great wound in Dorghar's flank before a backhand swing of the Everchosen's blade took off his skull. Karash, his Liege-Immortis, exchanged a flurry of blows with the lord of the Eightpoints but was soon bitten in half by the tyrant's daemonic beast.

The Mortarch's attendants dropped their accoutrements of service and hurled themselves at the Everchosen in defence of their master; one by one, they met a violent end. Finally, only the Mortarch remained.

Katakros shrugged off his robe and stepped forwards.

'Know that your end will be a slow and torturous one, trespasser,' growled Archaon.

Katakros merely raised his ensorcelled shield and awaited his enemy's strike.

The tyrant's mount struck with fearsome swiftness. Katakros fended off the slavering jaws of one chimeric head with the Shield Immortis and sank his glaive into the beast's neck.

As the beast reared away, Archaon slammed his burning blade into the Mortarch's shoulder, gouging through bone and armour. Katakros ducked aside as that dread sword lashed out again and again, each subsequent blow missing him by mere inches.

And so it went: strike, parry and cleaving blow, a duel of impossible speed and fury.

Here, before the gates of the Varanspire, there could be only one victor. Dorghar struck, and Katakros raised the Shield Immortis a fraction too slowly. Monstrous reptilian jaws clamped around his chest. He felt them crunch through his armoured body, agony searing through him as acidic drool poured into his form.

Another head clamped down and tore Inda-Khaat from his grasp.

Impaled and helpless, the Mortarch was lifted bodily to meet the pitiless, burning gaze of the Everchosen.

'Not… so easy,' Katakros gasped.

Then the Slayer of Kings descended and blackness consumed him.

As the Siege of the Eightpoints reached its fateful conclusion, Mortarch Katakros and the last of his dwindling armies faced the untrammelled might of Archaon the Everchosen's ruinous host.

DEATHLESS GLORY

The Battle of the Varanspire ended in the obliteration of the Ossiarch Bonereapers' vast army and the destruction of Mortarch Katakros at the hands of Archaon. But Death is eternal, and it cannot so easily be denied. The Arx Terminus still loomed over the Endgate, and within its ossified halls, an ancient evil regathered its strength.

At the top of the highest tower of the Arx Terminus was a vaulted hall sculpted from crystallised bone as black as night. Great pillars lined the room, each intricately and painstakingly carved with images of battle – faceless mortal hordes kneeling in supplication before a towering titan, ships burning amidst a bay of ice and a thousand other glorious depictions of victory. Skulls of various shapes and sizes were embedded in the walls, baleful emerald light spilling from their eye sockets.

Rising from the centre of the hall was a throne of stark, white bone, upon which sat the instigator of all these triumphs, the being to whom the architecture of the macabre palace paid glorious testament.

Mortarch Katakros was deep in thought. Before the skeletal tyrant, etched onto the floor tiles with glowing sigils, lay a map of the Eightpoints, a colossal eight-pointed star representing the Varanspire at its centre. Stooped necro-thralls pushed blocks of polished ivory and obsidian across its gleaming surface. Scrollbearers and signatories lined the hall, and carrion messenger birds were dispatched far and wide, exiting from gargoyle-mouthed portals carved into the ceiling.

'The Null Myriad to advance to the Screaming Mountain and lay siege to the Vornskar Dreadhold,' the Mortarch said. 'Praetorian echelons five hundred and four hundred and thirty to fortify Impaler's Pass. Siege towers to be raised and installed with sufficient Crawlers in order to saturate both banks of the Black River with artillery barrages.'

His Gnosis Scrollbearers began furiously etching each order upon slates of bone.

'The enemy will utilise the arterial roads to hasten their advance. Send word to Nagashizzar. I require spectral reinforcements in great numbers to sweep the armoured highways and disrupt the foe's movements. They must not be allowed a moment's peace.'

Katakros placed a hand upon the smooth ivory of his chestplate. There was pain still. That was strange. The process of osseomantic transferral should have eliminated every injury inflicted upon his previous form. Yet his chest still burned where the three-eyed one had plunged his fiery blade through armour and bone, sundering the necromantic magic that held the Mortarch's frame together.

The Everchosen had been as worthy a foe as the Mortarch had hoped. Defeating him would be a crowning glory to outrank any event depicted in the carvings of this chamber.

Katakros dismissed the agony. It was nothing new to him, merely another distraction to be conquered.

He rose from his throne and his Mornial attendants fell to their knees, prostrating themselves before the glory of their master. Two skittered forwards and lifted the hem of his robe as he strode to the rear of the chamber, where an immense stained-shadeglass window bled sickly purple light into the hall. Beyond, Katakros could see the misty haze of the Endgate.

Even now, his foremost Mortisan architects were securing the arcway with more interlocking networks of ballista towers and defensive trenches. Katakros was not prepared to take any chances – even should the enemy breach the Arx Terminus, his Ossiarchs would be able to fall back to this secondary set of fortifications and bleed the besiegers yet further.

The Mortarch of the Necropolis knew that the Battle of the Varanspire – while not a defeat in his mind – would not be the last time the enemy hurled their full might against him in an attempt to drive the armies of Nagash from their dominion. He greatly anticipated the next such encounter, for he had learnt many a lesson by observing the Everchosen's headlong ferocity. That had been the point of the campaign, after all.

Katakros passed through a great arch of polished bone and entered a sub-chamber limned with the viridian glow of soul-magic.

Here, more sculptor thralls skittered to and fro, their insectile, many-legged forms designed by their Mortisan masters purely to carry out the process of osseous craftsmanship.

Phossos awaited the Mortarch. Rising from his work-shrine, the Boneshaper gave a stiff bow.

'Lord Mortarch,' he rasped. 'Much progress has been made.'

Katakros did not acknowledge the master crafter. Instead, he studied the statues that littered the chamber – grand, imposing figures that were still being polished and refined by scores of hooded bone masons.

Each of the sculptures bore the noble image of Katakros the Undefeated.

'I will have need of many forms,' said Katakros. 'The first blow has been struck, but this war will not be won swiftly – nor without sacrifice.'

'You will have all that you require, master,' said Phossos. 'All and more. I promise you this: no blade or spell shall lay you low.'

Katakros nodded, satisfied.

'All proceeds as I have predicted,' he said. 'The Eightpoints will fall, as is the will of Great Nagash.'

PANOPLY OF CHAOS

Whether you are a master of the brush with decades of experience or you have never painted a Citadel Miniature in your life, the prospect of painting an army of the Dark Gods offers a unique and exciting challenge. The pages that follow contain some tips and examples to get you started with painting your own Chaos horde.

There is nothing quite like the sight of a fully painted army of Citadel Miniatures. There is real satisfaction to be had in adding your chosen colours, teasing out the finely sculpted details and truly making your miniatures collection your own. After all, one fully painted Chaos Warrior looks great, but an entire army of the damned brought together through shared colours is something even more fantastic. For those of us who are completionists, there is also immense gratification in watching your collection grow.

There is no right or wrong way to go about painting your collection of miniatures. Some people revel in treating each miniature as a work of art, lavishing attention on every millimetre of every model and painstakingly crafting scenic bases. Others prefer a far simpler approach with basic paint jobs that allow them to quickly assemble legions of finished models. And, of course, there is plenty of middle ground for those who enjoy painting their troops but want to devote special attention to key figures such as heroes, war machines and monsters.

The garish hosts of the Dark Gods are endlessly varied in colour and appearance, and the Citadel Miniatures in this range are packed with details for you to pick out. On the following pages, you will find a guide to painting the Chaos forces represented in this book. Remember, there is no one way to paint. Feel free to use these tips as inspiration for your own unique paint scheme!

WARHAMMER TV

Warhammer TV's painting tutorials have insights for everyone as they show you how to paint Citadel Miniatures from start to finish. The guides are available for free on games-workshop.com and can also be watched via the Warhammer TV YouTube channel. Why not take a moment to check them out?

BE'LAKOR'S SKIN

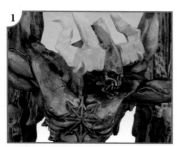

1 Over an undercoat of Grey Seer, paint all of Be'lakor's skin with Basilicanum Grey. Be careful not to overload the brush as the paint may pool.

2 Black Templar is then applied to the darker areas of the skin. Add Contrast Medium when painting the graduated areas.

3 Using the previous coats of Contrast paint as a guide, apply a layer of Dawnstone to the lighter grey areas and an edge highlight to the black areas.

4 Apply a layer of Administratum Grey to the light grey areas (drybrushing the wings) and an edge highlight to the black areas.

5 Use Grey Seer to highlight the light grey elements and add reflective dots to the black areas.

TOP TIP

It is good practice to apply a coat of Munitorum Varnish or Stormshield to your models to protect them against the wear and tear of battle!

BE'LAKOR'S DETAILS

Base: Brass Scorpion.
Shade: Agrax Earthshade.
Layer: Brass Scorpion.
Edge Highlight:
Runefang Steel.

Base: Skavenblight Dinge.
Shade: Nuln Oil.
Edge Highlight:
Stormvermin Fur,
Administratum Grey.

Base: Rhinox Hide.
Highlight: XV-88,
Ushabti Bone.

Base: Iron Hands Steel.
Shade: Nuln Oil.
Drybrush: Runefang Steel.

BE'LAKOR'S SWORD

Apply a basecoat of Iron Hands Steel, then shade with Nuln Oil. Add a highlight of Iron Hands Steel before finishing with an edge highlight of Runefang Steel.

FACIAL DETAILS

Teeth: Corax White.

Eyes: Evil Sunz Scarlet followed by a dot of Yriel Yellow.

Tongue: Screamer Pink with a highlight of Kakophoni Purple.

BE'LAKOR'S DAEMON LEGION BANNER

1

Using slightly thinned Corax White, paint a circle onto your banner. Use Abaddon Black (the field colour) to tidy up any mistakes.

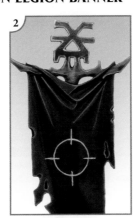

2

Draw short lines, first down the centre of the circle, then horizontally across. It's important to build up freehand work in systematic increments.

3

Next, draw shorter lines in between the lines that you previously painted for a total of eight. This forms a strong base for your icon.

4

Carefully broaden the lines, then add arrows to the tips by painting 'V' shapes and filling them in. This creates the iconic Chaos Star motif.

THE FLAYED - ARMOUR

1 Apply an undercoat of Wraithbone.

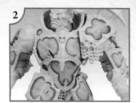

2 Paint with a 1:1 mix of Skeleton Horde and Contrast Medium. You can leave it here for a Battle Ready finish.

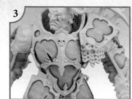

3 Layer the armour with a couple of thin coats of Ushabti Bone.

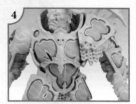

4 Edge highlight the armour with White Scar. Use Ushabti Bone to tidy up if you need to.

THE FLAYED - DETAILS

Base: Retributor Armour.
Contrast: Guilliman Flesh.
Edge Highlight: Runefang Steel.

Base: Wraithbone.
Contrast: Guilliman Flesh.
Highlight: Pallid Wych Flesh.

Base: Leadbelcher.
Shade: Nuln Oil.
Edge Highlight: Runefang Steel.
Add small dashes to give the effect of scratches.

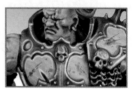

Apply dashes and dots of Blood For The Blood God to create a blood spatter effect on the armour.

THE BALEFUL LORDS - SKIN

1 Apply an undercoat of Mephiston Red.

2 Apply a 2:1 mix of Contrast Medium and Flesh Tearers Red.

3 Drybrush with Evil Sunz Scarlet.

4 Edge highlight with Fire Dragon Bright, or drybrush for a quicker result.

THE BALEFUL LORDS - DETAILS

Eyes: Basecoat with Abaddon Black, layer with Yriel Yellow and add dots of Abaddon Black for the pupils.

Teeth: Basecoat with Abaddon Black, then highlight with Dawnstone, painting a line around the edge of each tooth for a sharp, glistening effect.

Tongue: Basecoat with Abaddon Black, apply a layer of Screamer Pink then highlight with Pink Horror.

Basecoat with Abaddon Black, drybrush with Skavenblight Dinge (tidying up with Abaddon Black), then edge highlight with Dawnstone.

Basecoat with Abaddon Black, then apply edge highlights of Incubi Darkness followed by Dawnstone.

THE UNBOUND FLUX - SKIN

1
Apply an undercoat of Grey Seer.

2
Paint the skin with a 1:2 mix of Volupus Pink and Contrast Medium for a Battle Ready finish.

3
Apply a layer of Emperor's Children.

4
Edge highlight with Fulgrim Pink.

THE UNBOUND FLUX - DETAILS

Tongue: Over a basecoat of Grey Seer, apply Terradon Turquoise. Layer with Temple Guard then highlight with Blue Horror.

Eyes: Basecoat with Abaddon Black then apply Moot Green, making sure the recesses remain dark.

Teeth: Basecoat with Abaddon Black, layer with Incubi Darkness then highlight with Dawnstone.

Paint Iyanden Yellow over Grey Seer. Shade the bottom half of the feathers with Fuegan Orange then edge highlight with Screaming Skull.

Apply Warp Lightning over Grey Seer. Layer with Moot Green and highlight with Yriel Yellow.

THE CULT OF A THOUSAND EYES - SKIN AND DETAILS

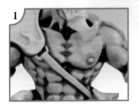

1
Over a Grey Seer undercoat, paint the skin with Gryph-charger Grey. You can leave it here for a Battle Ready finish.

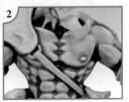

2
Apply a highlight of Ulthuan Grey.

Base: Grey Seer.
Contrast: Black Templar.
Highlight: Dawnstone.

Base: Grey Seer.
Contrast: Apothecary White.
Layer: Corax White.
Highlight: White Scar.

THE CULT OF A THOUSAND EYES - ARMOUR

1
Over a Grey Seer undercoat, paint the shield with Terradon Turquoise, being careful not to let it pool.

2
Apply Incubi Darkness to the field of the shield. You can leave it here for a Battle Ready finish.

3
Edge highlight the trim and details of the shield with Administratum Grey.

Base: Castellax Bronze.
Shade: Reikland Fleshshade Gloss.
Edge Highlight: Stormhost Silver.

THE MUNIFICENT WANDERERS - SKIN AND BUBOES

Apply an undercoat of Grey Seer.

Paint with a 1:1 mix of Militarum Green and Contrast Medium for a Battle Ready finish.

Drybrush with Grey Seer.

Shade the buboes with Carroburg Crimson then apply a layer of Ungor Flesh.

THE MUNIFICENT WANDERERS - DETAILS

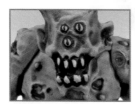

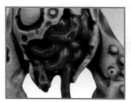

Over a coat of Wyldwood, paint the eyes Yriel Yellow with a line of Abaddon Black for the pupils. Add a layer of Screaming Skull to the teeth.

Paint the guts with Bugman's Glow, then add a coat of Blood For The Blood God.

Over a Grey Seer undercoat, apply a coat of Wyldwood. Stipple with Ryza Rust then add an edge highlight of Runefang Steel.

Apply a coat of Wyldwood, then add edge highlights of Gorthor Brown and Karak Stone.

THE DRONING GUARD - ROT FLY BODY

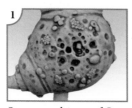

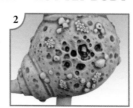

Over an undercoat of Grey Seer, paint with a 1:1 mix of Guilliman Flesh and Contrast Medium for a Battle Ready finish.

Drybrush the skin with Pallid Wych Flesh.

Add Iyanden Yellow to the buboes and Blood For The Blood God to the wounds, drawing some streaks to create dribbles of gore.

The Plaguebearers of the Droning Guard have the same sickly pale skin as their mounts.

THE DRONING GUARD - DETAILS

Base: Rhinox Hide.
Shade: Nuln Oil.
Edge Highlight: Gorthor Brown, Karak Stone.

Base: Grey Seer.
Contrast: Terradon Turquoise.
Drybrush: Ulthuan Grey.

For the eyes, paint with Abaddon Black and add a layer of 'Ardcoat. For the teeth, apply Wyldwood and layer with Wraithbone.

Base: Leadbelcher.
Contrast: Basilicanum Grey.
Edge Highlight: Runefang Steel.

THE BLESSED SONS - SKIN

1 Over a Grey Seer undercoat, apply a 1:1 mix of Guilliman Flesh and Contrast Medium.

2 Drybrush the skin with Pallid Wych Flesh, slowly building up to the desired finish.

3 Apply a 1:1 mix of Carroburg Crimson and Contrast Medium to the sore areas of skin.

4 Paint the buboes with Nurgles Rot and add Blood For The Blood God to the wounds.

THE BLESSED SONS - GREEN ARMOUR

1 Apply 2 coats of Militarum Green over a Grey Seer undercoat, allowing each coat to dry thoroughly. You can leave it here for a Battle Ready finish.

2 Edge highlight the armour with Elysian Green. This will help to bring out the detail of the armour panels.

3 Apply a further, slightly finer edge highlight of Ogryn Camo.

Base: Brass Scorpion.
Shade: Reikland Fleshshade Gloss.
Highlight: Runefang Steel.
Recess Shade: Nihilakh Oxide.

THE DROWNED MEN - ROT FLY BODY

1 Over a Grey Seer undercoat, apply a coat of Plaguebearer Flesh for a Battle Ready finish.

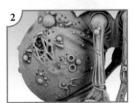
2 Drybrush the skin with Pallid Wych Flesh.

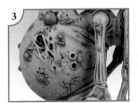
3 Paint the buboes with Nazdreg Yellow and add Blood For The Blood God to the wounds.

Base: Abaddon Black.
Edge Highlight: Incubi Darkness, Dawnstone.

THE DROWNED MEN - DETAILS

Base: Grey Seer.
Contrast: Gryph-charger Grey.
Drybrush: Ulthuan Grey.

Base: Lupercal Green.
Recess Shade: Nuln Oil.
Edge Highlight: Sons of Horus Green, Administratum Grey.

Base: Brass Scorpion.
Shade: Agrax Earthshade Gloss.
Edge Highlight: Stormhost Silver.

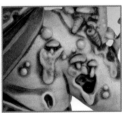
Base: Grey Seer.
Contrast: Gryph-charger Grey.
Highlight: Grey Seer.

THE SCARLET CAVALCADE - SEEKER SKIN AND FINS

1

Over a Grey Seer undercoat, apply a 1:1 shade of Carroburg Crimson and Contrast Medium.

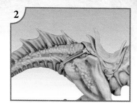

2

Apply a light drybrush of Pallid Wych Flesh, followed by a layer of Pallid Wych Flesh to smooth it out.

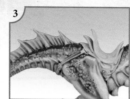

3

Apply a 1:1 mix of Blood For The Blood God and Lahmian Medium onto the scaly texture and stipple it out over the skin.

4

Basecoat the fins with Abaddon Black, highlight with Khorne Red, then add an edge highlight of Pink Horror.

THE SCARLET CAVALCADE - DETAILS

Follow the first two steps for the Seeker Skin above, adding Blood For The Blood God to the face as gory warpaint.

Base: Grey Seer.
Contrast: Apothecary White.
Highlight: White Scar.

Base: Gal Vorbak Red.
Shade: Nuln Oil.
Edge Highlight: Wazdakka Red, Pink Horror.

Base: Khorne Red.
Recess Shade: Nuln Oil.
Edge Highlight: Evil Sunz Scarlet, Fire Dragon Bright.

THE FAULTLESS BLADES - SKIN

1

Apply an undercoat of Grey Seer.

2

Paint the skin with Black Templar. You can leave it here for a Battle Ready finish.

3

Highlight with Dawnstone.

4

Paint the eyes with Evil Sunz Scarlet and add a dot of Fire Dragon Bright. Paint the teeth with Pallid Wych Flesh.

THE FAULTLESS BLADES - DETAILS

Base: Grey Knights Steel.
Contrast: Magos Purple.
Edge Highlight: Stormhost Silver.

Base: Grey Seer.
Contrast: Magos Purple.
Drybrush: Grey Seer.

Base: Grey Seer.
Contrast: Shyish Purple.
Edge Highlight: Kakophoni Purple.

Base: Retributor Armour.
Shade: Reikland Fleshshade Gloss.
Edge Highlight: Stormhost Silver.

THE LURID HAZE – SKIN

1

Apply an undercoat of Grey Seer.

2

Paint the skin with Magos Purple. You can leave it here for a Battle Ready finish.

3

Highlight with Grey Seer.

4

Paint the eyes with Abaddon Black followed by 'Ardcoat. Apply Carroburg Crimson around the eyes.

THE LURID HAZE – DETAILS

Base: Grey Seer.
Contrast: Volupus Pink (2 coats).
Drybrush: Emperor's Children.

Base: Grey Seer.
Contrast: Gryph-hound Orange.
Edge Highlight: Fire Dragon Bright.

Base: Abaddon Black.
Edge Highlight: Stegadon Scale Green, Sons of Horus Green.

Base: Grey Seer.
Contrast: Iyanden Yellow, stippling Gryph-hound Orange at the bottom.
Highlight: Screaming Skull.

ENVIRONMENTS OF THE EIGHTPOINTS

Apply Stirland Battlemire with an M Texture tool. Once dry, drybrush with Mournfang Brown then Karak Stone.
Paint the Barbed Bracken separately by applying an undercoat of Wraithbone and layering with Iyanden Yellow. Attach them to the base with superglue and add some Middenland Tufts.

Apply Mordant Earth thickly to the base (it might be worth testing it out on a spare base first), then paint the stones with Abaddon Black. Drybrush the whole base with Incubi Darkness, going heavier over the stones, then apply Administratum Grey in the same manner. Finally, add small patches of Valhallan Blizzard.

Apply patches of Martian Iron Crust, then paint the rest of the base with Martian Ironearth. Paint the rocks with Mechanicus Standard Grey and shade with Agrax Earthshade. Drybrush the whole base with Karak Stone. Apply streaks of Blood For The Blood God.

Apply Agrellan Earth to the base. Paint the skulls with Wraithbone, then add a coat of Skeleton Horde. Drybrush the whole base with Wraithbone, going heavier over the skulls. Finally, add some Mordheim Turf.

BONE-TITHE NEXUS – SKELETONS

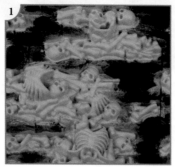

1

Over a Chaos Black undercoat, apply a couple of coats of Morghast Bone to the mounds of skeletons using an M Base brush.

2

Next, apply a shade of Seraphim Sepia over the bones, allowing it to settle into the deepest recesses.

3

Drybrush the skeletons with Ushabti Bone.

4

Apply a final drybrush of Wraithbone to the skeletons to give them a sun-bleached finish and bring out the detail.

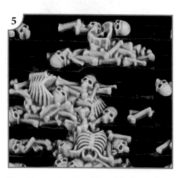

5

Finally, apply Abaddon Black to the black areas, tidying up the inevitable mess you made when drybrushing the skeletons.

TOP TIP

Drybrushing is a fantastic technique for painting scenery, as it is quick and effective. There are, however, certain procedures that should be followed to achieve the desired result.

1. Apply a small amount of paint to your brush.

2. Remove most of the paint from your brush with a paper towel, working it into the bristles.

3. Draw the brush repeatedly across the surface of the model, catching the details and edges to avoid streaking on the flat surfaces.

BONE-TITHE NEXUS – BLACK STONE

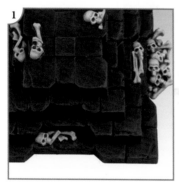

1

Using an S Dry brush, apply a drybrush of Eshin Grey, being careful to avoid the bone. Focus your drybrushing as best you can on the edges of the stone.

2

Next, apply a drybrush of Dawnstone to the edges of the stone. If you like, on some of the sharper panels, you can apply this as an edge highlight instead.

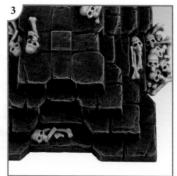

3

If you want more definition, a gentle drybrush of Grey Seer will help to bring out the most extreme edges of the stonework.

BONE-TITHE NEXUS – BONE

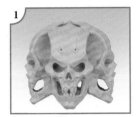

1

Apply a basecoat of Morghast Bone.

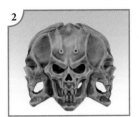

2

Apply a 1:1 mix of Agrax Earthshade and Lahmian Medium.

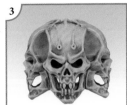

3

Add a few thin layers of Ushabti Bone to the raised areas, avoiding the recesses.

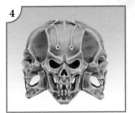

4

Apply an edge highlight of White Scar.

BONE-TITHE NEXUS – GREY BONE

1

Apply a basecoat of Mechanicus Standard Grey.

2

Shade with a 1:1 mix of Nuln Oil and Lahmian Medium.

3

Layer with Dawnstone.

4

Highlight with Administratum Grey.

BONE-TITHE NEXUS – WOODEN BARRELS

1

Apply a basecoat of Rhinox Hide.

2

Drybrush with Mournfang Brown.

3

Drybrush with Balor Brown.

4

Metal Binding: Basecoat with Leadbelcher, shade with Nuln Oil, highlight with Runefang Steel.

BONE-TITHE NEXUS – DETAILS

Base: Incubi Darkness.
Layer: Kabalite Green.
Edge Highlight: Moot Green.
Recess Shade: Moot Green

Base: Steel Legion Drab.
Shade: Agrax Earthshade.
Highlight: Karak Stone

Base: Abaddon Black.
Highlight: Dark Reaper, Thunderhawk Blue, Blue Horror.

TOP TIP

When edge highlighting, you should try to make each subsequent line finer than the last. This gives the effect of a gradient towards a sharp edge.

If you're just starting out, it's a good idea to do just one edge highlight; then, when you are more practised, you can go back and add more.

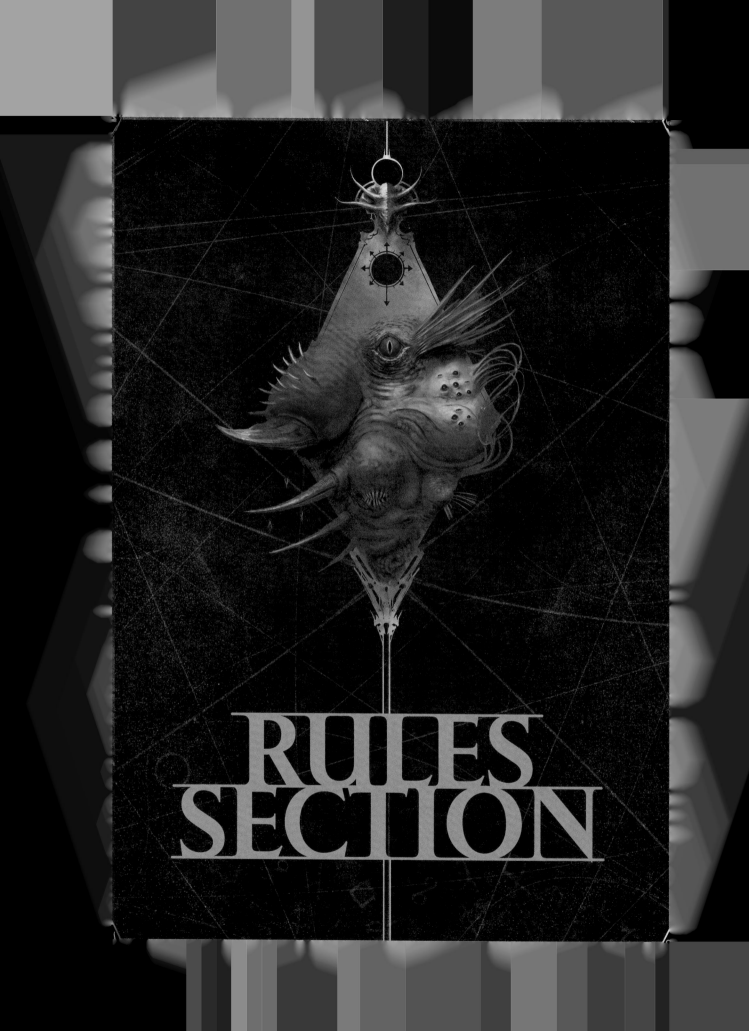

RULES
SECTION

Upon the bloodstained fields of the Eightpoints, the armies of Archaon the Everchosen and Mortarch Katakros come together in a clash of shattering violence. Grand fortresses are besieged, their walls scaled in a storm of blood and fire as the relentless volleys of siege engines pummel and pulverise stone and bodies alike. Sweeping packs of sentient spells roar across the land, devouring or immolating all in their path, while nightmarish monstrosities are drawn forth from their lairs, awoken by the crash of blades and the scent of boundless slaughter.

The Warhammer Age of Sigmar tabletop game is your gateway to this fantastical world of warfare and cataclysmic magic, where savage champions and valiant heroes clash in furious battle. On the following pages, you will find a host of rules for expanding your Age of Sigmar experience, with a focus on recreating the raging battles for the fate of the Eightpoints. Everything in this section is intended to be used in conjunction with the core rules presented in the *Warhammer Age of Sigmar Core Book*, supplementing that easy-to-learn system with many exciting additional options for the three pillars of the game: narrative, matched and open play.

To begin, you will find a selection of rules designed to allow you to create your own thrilling stories through narrative play. Realm of Battle rules reflect the horrendous experience of combat in the Eightpoints, a land utterly saturated with Chaos magic. As well as unique spells and command abilities befitting those who hail from this dread land, there are rules that represent the deadly environs themselves, from lashing storms of boiling blood to strange and intoxicating melodies that imbue the listener with an unquenchable desire to destroy their foes.

Rules for Roaming Monsters and wandering endless spells add an extra layer of unpredictability to your games, reflecting the notoriously anarchic nature of the Everchosen's domain. In addition, full rules for Siege Warfare allow you to experience challenging, asymmetrical battles to control the many fortresses and strongholds of the Mortal Realms – individual abilities for attackers and defenders are provided for every faction in the game.

Eight unique battleplans will allow you to recreate the most infamous of the titanic clashes between the forces of Death and Chaos, as recounted in the story told in this book. Though these are designed to bring to life the ferocious struggles that took place across the Chaos-ravaged plains of Archaon's domain, they are intended to be compatible with any army you might wish to field and can take place anywhere against the endlessly varied backdrop of the Eight Realms.

Finally, you will find new allegiance abilities for the varied fighting forces under the Everchosen's command, from dark daemonic hosts to blood-crazed Bloodbound hordes and twisted worshippers of the Dark Prince Slaanesh.

DANGER AT EVERY TURN

The Eightpoints is a land of nightmares, dotted with jagged keeps of cursed stone and ravaged by abominable monsters, voracious sentient magic and reaving tribes sworn to the Dark Gods. To make war in such a place is to fight in one of the most inhospitable environments imaginable.

This section contains exciting new rules that you can use to recreate the battles that raged across the Eightpoints during the invasion of Mortarch Katakros, including Realm of Battle, Roaming Monsters and Siege Warfare rules as well as wandering endless spells.

These rules have been designed with narrative play in mind. They encourage a thematic style of play that will enable you to create your own thrilling stories of anarchic battles fought in the heartlands of Chaos, but you could easily combine them with rules provided in the *Warhammer Age of Sigmar: Core Book* to represent ferocious battles fought elsewhere in the Mortal Realms.

REALM OF BATTLE
This section includes Region of War rules to fight battles set in the Eightpoints. Realmsphere magic, realm commands and realmscape features provide rules to represent the chaotic plains around the Varanspire (pg 63).

ROAMING MONSTERS
New rules that allow players to add wild monsters to games of Warhammer Age of Sigmar (pg 64-65).

WANDERING ENDLESS SPELLS
New endless spell rules available for games of Warhammer Age of Sigmar set in the Eightpoints (pg 66-68).

SIEGE WARFARE
Updated Siege Warfare rules with new allegiance abilities for each faction in Warhammer Age of Sigmar (pg 70-75).

BATTLEPLANS
This section includes new narrative battleplans that can be played to recreate the story of Katakros' invasion (pg 76-83).

REALM OF BATTLE
REGION OF WAR: THE EIGHTPOINTS

The following rules can be used for battles fought in the island sub-realm of the Eightpoints. These rules work especially well for battles that include Roaming Monsters and wandering endless spells.

REALMSPHERE MAGIC

WIZARDS know the following spell in battles fought in this region in addition to any other spells that they know.

Marked Quarry: *The wizard conjures a shroud of luminescent energy over the foe that draws the attention of nearby beasts.*

Marked Quarry has a casting value of 7. If successfully cast, pick 1 enemy unit within 18" of the caster and visible to them. Until the start of your next hero phase, Roaming Monsters units must make any charge moves or normal moves (excluding retreat moves) towards that unit, and any shooting attacks made by Roaming Monsters units must target that unit, even if that unit is not the closest unit to the Roaming Monsters unit.

REALM COMMANDS

You can use the following command abilities in battles fought in this region in addition to the command abilities that you are normally allowed to use.

Forced by the Aether: *The shaman adds momentum to the endless spells on the battlefield so that they cover greater distances.*

You can use this command ability when you pick a predatory endless spell to move. If you do so, pick 1 predatory endless spell within 12" of a friendly **WIZARD**. Add D6" to the movement range on that predatory endless spell's warscroll until the end of the battle round.

REALMSCAPE FEATURES

If a battle takes place in this region, the player who picked the realm can roll a dice and look up the result on the table below to see which realmscape feature rule applies for the battle. The result applies to both players.

D6   Realmscape Feature

1   The Gods Hold No Interest Here: *The Ruinous Powers have deemed there is too little at stake to entertain this conflict.*

This realmscape feature has no effect on the battle.

2   Furious Bloodstorm: *Scalding crimson rain lashes down across the battlefield, inspiring a mindless rage in all it touches.*

Subtract 1 from casting rolls for **WIZARDS**. In addition, you can re-roll wound rolls of 1 for attacks made with melee weapons by units that made a charge move in the same turn.

3   Drifting Chokespores: *A nearby copse of mouldering trees vomits clouds of toxic spores into the air, severely limiting sight and movement.*

Units cannot fly. In addition, subtract 1 from hit rolls for attacks made with missile weapons.

4   Crystal Wyrdshards: *Fragments from Tzeentch's realm have rained down upon the Eightpoints. Those who wield the arcane can drink from these pure fonts of magic – at their own risk, of course.*

You can re-roll casting rolls for **WIZARDS** on the battlefield. However, if a casting attempt is re-rolled using this rule and is successful, that **WIZARD** suffers D3 mortal wounds after the effects of the spell have been resolved.

5   Exultant Melody: *A soul-piercing note rings out across the battlefield, igniting the senses of all who hear it.*

Units can run and still charge later in the same turn. However, any units that run and charge in the same turn suffer D3 mortal wounds at the end of the charge phase.

6   The Great Game: *The Gods wager on the victor of this conflict, each lending their power to the battlefield to tip the scales in their favour.*

At the start of each battle round, before determining which player has the first turn, the players roll off. The winner decides which 1 of the following realmscape features will be used for that battle round: Furious Bloodstorm, Drifting Chokespores, Crystal Wyrdshards or Exultant Melody.

ROAMING MONSTERS

The Mortal Realms are home to all kinds of terrible abominations, beings twisted by magic or corruption into hideous, predatory forms. Such creatures know no allegiance beyond their own ravening hunger, and their appearance upon the battlefield heralds a bloodbath of terrible proportions.

If players agree beforehand, the following rules for Roaming Monsters can be used in a Warhammer Age of Sigmar battle.

After armies have been set up but before the first battle round begins, the players roll off. Starting with the winner, players alternate picking units one at a time from the following list:

- 1 Chaos Gargant
- 1 Chimera
- 1 Cockatrice
- 1 Cygor
- 1 Fomoroid Crusher
- 1 Ghorgon
- 1 Jabberslythe
- 1 Mindstealer Sphiranx
- 1 Mutalith Vortex Beast
- 1 Slaughterbrute
- 1 Soul Grinder
- 1 unit of 10 Chaos Warhounds

- 1 unit of 6 Furies
- 1 unit of 6 Raptoryx
- 1 unit of 3 Razorgors

These units are not part of either player's army and are referred to as 'Roaming Monsters' in the rules that follow.

Once they have picked a Roaming Monsters unit, the player must set it up on the battlefield within 1" of a terrain feature and more than 9" from any units in either player's army.

The total number of Roaming Monsters units set up on the battlefield cannot exceed the total number of artefacts of power in both players' armies combined. If neither player has any artefacts of power, only 1 Roaming Monsters unit can be set up on the battlefield.

Roaming Monsters units are treated as enemy units by both players' armies, and Roaming Monsters units treat all units except other Roaming Monsters units as enemy units.

PRIMAL INSTINCTS

Roaming Monsters units are activated at the start of each battle round, after any endless spells have been moved but before the first turn begins. The players alternate picking 1 Roaming Monsters unit to activate, starting with the player who has the second turn. Each Roaming Monsters unit can be activated once per battle round. To do so, roll a dice and consult the behaviour table opposite. The behaviour table has 3 columns, each with 6 results. The distance between the Roaming Monsters unit and the closest enemy models determines which column you use.

BEHAVIOUR TABLE

D6	IN COMBAT *Within 3" of any enemy models.*	CLOSE *Between 3" and 12" from any enemy models.*	FAR *More than 12" from any enemy models.*
1	Distracted	Distracted	Distracted
2	Spooked	Hold	Hold
3	Hold	Hold	Hold
4	Hold	Charge	Advance
5	Hold	Charge	Advance
6	Rampage	Charge	Advance

ACTIONS

Each roll on the behaviour table has a corresponding action that the Roaming Monsters unit will perform. These actions have numbered steps that must be resolved immediately in the order they appear by the player activating the unit before the next Roaming Monsters unit can be activated.

Many of the actions require the players to determine the closest model or closest unit. If there are two or more eligible models or units, the player activating the Roaming Monsters unit picks which one will be treated as the closest for the purpose of that action.

DISTRACTED

1. This unit does nothing.

SPOOKED

1. This unit must retreat. If it cannot do so for any reason, it is destroyed.

HOLD

1. This unit can use 1 ability from its warscroll (if it is able to do so).

2. If this unit has any missile weapons, it can shoot. All attacks must target the closest enemy unit.

ADVANCE

1. This unit can use 1 ability from its warscroll (if it is able to do so).

2. This unit makes a normal move. Each model from this unit must finish the move as close as possible to the closest enemy unit.

3. If this unit has any missile weapons, it can shoot. All attacks must target the closest enemy unit.

CHARGE

1. This unit makes a normal move. Each model from this unit must finish the move as close as possible to the closest enemy unit.

2. If this unit has any missile weapons, it can shoot. All attacks must target the closest enemy unit.

3. This unit attempts to make a charge move towards the closest enemy unit.

4. If the first model moved can finish its charge move within ½" of the closest enemy unit, it does so, moving as close as possible to that enemy unit, and the charge is successful. Otherwise, the charge fails and no models from this unit move.

5. If the charge is successful, each model from this unit must finish the charge move as close as possible to the closest enemy unit.

RAMPAGE

1. This unit can use 1 ability from its warscroll (if it is able to do so).

2. If this unit has any missile weapons, it can shoot. All attacks must target the closest enemy unit.

3. Each enemy unit within 1" of any models from this unit suffers D3 mortal wounds.

THE COMBAT PHASE

At the start of each combat phase, before any eligible units from either player's army have been picked to fight, the players take it in turns to pick Roaming Monsters units to fight, starting with the player whose turn is taking place. A Roaming Monsters unit must be within 3" of a unit from a player's army to be picked to fight.

Once a Roaming Monsters unit has been picked, identify which model from a player's army is closest to that unit. This model is referred to as their quarry. If two or more models are eligible, the player who picked the unit to fight chooses which one will be their quarry.

Each model in that Roaming Monsters unit piles in towards their quarry and attacks the unit it belongs to with all of its melee weapons that are in range.

ALLOCATING WOUNDS

When allocating wounds to a Roaming Monsters unit, the player whose turn is taking place chooses which model in the unit to allocate the wounds to (with any restrictions that normally apply).

If a Roaming Monsters unit suffers wounds outside of either player's turn, the players roll off and the winner chooses which model in the unit to allocate the wounds to.

Do not take battleshock tests for Roaming Monsters units.

At the end of any turn, if a Roaming Monsters unit is split into two or more groups, no models are removed from that unit. Instead, the next time that unit makes any kind of move, the models must reform back into a single group. If they are unable to do so, that unit cannot move.

WANDERING ENDLESS SPELLS

Ever since the dawn of the Arcanum Optimar, when the arcane laws of the cosmos were thrown into disarray, the realms have been plagued by eruptions of rogue magic – gatherings of sentient spells that sweep across the land in hunting packs, devouring or incinerating everything in their path.

If players agree beforehand, the following rules for wandering endless spells can be used in a Warhammer Age of Sigmar battle.

After armies and any Roaming Monsters have been set up, before the first battle round begins, the players roll off. Starting with the winner, the players alternate picking predatory endless spells one at a time to be included as wandering endless spells in the battle.

Predatory endless spell models and their warscrolls are available in the *Warhammer Age of Sigmar: Malign Sorcery* supplement, and further predatory endless spell warscrolls are available in some battletomes.

These models are not part of either player's army and are referred to as 'wandering endless spells' in the rules that follow.

Once they have picked a wandering endless spell, the player must set it up on the battlefield. To do so, roll a D3 and consult the map below. The result of the roll and the number of the current battle round determine which point on the map will be used. For example, if it is the first battle round and the player rolls a 2, they would use the point in the centre of the battlefield.

Set up the wandering endless spell within 9" of that point and more than 6" from any units on the battlefield. Do not immediately make a move with the model,

even if one of the abilities on its warscroll would normally allow you to do so.

The total number of wandering endless spells set up on the battlefield cannot exceed the total number of artefacts of power in both players' armies combined. If neither player has any artefacts of power, only 1 wandering endless spell can be set up on the battlefield.

At the start of each battle round after the first, after all predatory endless spells have been moved, the players roll off. Starting with the winner, the players alternate setting up wandering endless spells following the same rules as before.

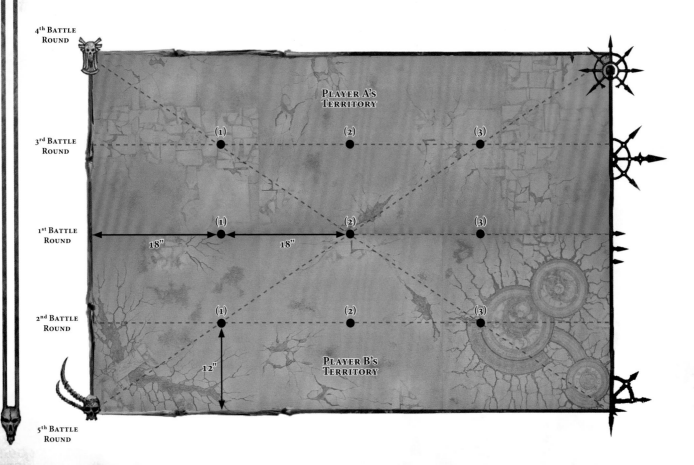

VOLATILE BY NATURE

Wandering endless spells work differently to normal predatory endless spells. They are activated after all predatory endless spells on the battlefield have been moved, before the first turn of the battle round begins. Unless otherwise stated, any effects and abilities on their warscrolls can be used as normal and are resolved by the player activating that wandering endless spell. The players alternate picking 1 wandering endless spell to activate, starting with the player who has the second turn.

Each wandering endless spell can be activated once per battle round. To do so, roll a D3 and consult the behaviour table below. The behaviour table has 3 columns, each with 6 results. The distance between the wandering endless spell model and the closest enemy models determines which column you use. Each roll on the behaviour table has a corresponding action that the wandering endless spell will perform. The action must be resolved immediately before the next wandering endless spell can be activated.

D6	IN COMBAT *Within 3" of any enemy models.*	CLOSE *Between 3" and 12" from any enemy models.*	FAR *More than 12" from any enemy models.*
1	Unstable	Surge	Translocation
2	Unstable	Surge	Translocation
3	Unleashed Power	Surge	Translocation
4	Unleashed Power	Surge	Translocation
5	Unleashed Power	Unleashed Power	Unleashed Power
6	Unleashed Power	Unleashed Power	Unleashed Power

BEHAVIOUR TABLE

UNSTABLE

The player activating the wandering endless spell rolls a dice. On a 1-3, the endless spell is immediately dispelled. On a 4-6, each unit within 3" of the endless spell suffers D3 mortal wounds.

TRANSLOCATION

The player activating the wandering endless spell rolls a dice. On a 1-2, nothing happens. On a 3+, the player removes the endless spell model from the battlefield and sets it up again on one of the points shown on the map opposite for the current battle round. If this is not possible, the endless spell model is removed from play.

UNLEASHED POWER

The player activating the wandering endless spell rolls on the Unleashed Power Effects table overleaf and immediately resolves the effects of the roll.

SURGE

The player activating the wandering endless spell must move the model as close as possible to the closest unit, finishing the move at least as close to the closest unit as it was at the start of the move. If there are two or more eligible units, the player activating the wandering endless spell picks which one will be treated as the closest for the purpose of that action.

The distance that the wandering endless spell can move will be noted on its warscroll, as well as any effects or abilities that activate when the model is moved.

FORMIDABLE TO BEHOLD

At the end of each battle round, starting with the player who took the second turn in that battle round, the players alternate picking 1 wandering endless spell on the battlefield and rolling on the Unleashed Power Effects table. After rolling on the table, the player immediately resolves the effects of the roll for that wandering endless spell and then removes the endless spell model from the battlefield (unless otherwise stated).

Unless noted otherwise, a wandering endless spell model cannot be attacked or affected by spells or abilities; it is treated as a friendly model by all armies for any other rules purposes.

UNLEASHED POWER EFFECTS	
D6	**Effect**
1	**Arcane Implosion:** Roll a dice for each unit within 18" of this wandering endless spell. On a 6, that unit suffers D6 mortal wounds.
2	**Temporal Distortion:** Roll a dice for each unit within 12" of this wandering endless spell. On a 6, remove that unit from the battlefield and set that unit up again anywhere on the battlefield more than 9" from any enemy units.
3	**Null Shockwave:** Mark the location of this wandering endless spell with a token before removing the model from the battlefield. Until the end of the next battle round, **WIZARDS** within 18" of that token cannot make casting, unbinding or dispelling rolls.
4	**Magical Fissure:** Place an identical wandering endless spell wholly within 6" of this wandering endless spell and more than 9" from any units. If it is the end of the battle round, do not remove these models from the battlefield. If it is not possible to set up an identical endless spell, resolve the effect for 'Arcane Implosion' instead.
5	**Transfigured Energy:** Replace this wandering endless spell with another from the Wandering Endless Spells table in the same position. If it is the end of the battle round, do not remove this model from the battlefield.
6	**Arcane Radiance:** Roll a dice for each unit on the battlefield. On a 5+, that unit suffers D3 mortal wounds.

In areas of the realms saturated with unstable magic, predatory spells form into unpredictable and deadly hunting packs, obliterating all in their path as they rampage across the land.

SIEGE WARFARE

Strongholds of all different shapes and sizes stud the Mortal Realms. Only a sizeable and highly motivated force has any chance of capturing one of these fortresses and laying claim to the spoils that lie beyond their walls – and only then at a terrible cost.

Assaulting a fortress is no small matter. Many have tall, strong walls covered with protective devices that are designed to punish any intruders, with garrisons of staunch defenders standing ready to rain death upon any attackers. Others are naturally occurring, such as an area of densely forested woodland or a series of ancient and long-abandoned caves, and can be used by a cunning or desperate defender to provide cover and stem an enemy assault.

The following rules allow you to fight a battle in which one player must assault an enemy stronghold and one must defend it. Also included are two Siege Warfare battleplans for you to use alongside these rules. Imaginative players will find it easy to modify the following rules for other types of siege battles.

THE STRONGHOLD

All Warhammer Age of Sigmar sieges require a stronghold for the Defender to occupy. As noted above, the exact nature of a stronghold varies a great deal; it might be an Awakened Wyldwood or a set of ancient ruins. Because of this, the Defender is given free rein to create their stronghold using any terrain features that they have available.

The Siege Warfare battleplan you choose for your battle will let you know how to pick the Attacker and the Defender. It will also tell you which of the territories they occupy at the start of the battle.

The scenery is set up in the Attacker's territory and any neutral areas of the battlefield as normal, and then the Defender must set up at least 5 terrain features wholly within their territory to represent their stronghold. There is no limit to the number of terrain features the Defender can use for their stronghold, provided that all the scenery fits wholly within their territory. You can choose any terrain features you like in your own battles, or you can use the examples shown in the *Warhammer Age of Sigmar Core Book* as inspiration.

Once the stronghold has been set up, the players then set up their armies as described in the battleplan they are using.

THE SIEGE PHASE

The siege phase takes place after the stronghold has been built and the armies have been set up but before the first battle round begins. It contains the siege tactics that the Attacker will use before the assault to wear down the Defender and the counter-tactics that the Defender will use to ensure they can hold out as long as possible.

SIEGE TACTICS

There are 3 main tactics that a besieging army will employ before the battle starts, each of which has a corresponding counter-tactic that the Defender will use against it.

Starve/Gather Supplies: The Attacker isolates the stronghold so that the Defender's army starves to death once their supplies begin to run out. The Defender counters this by gathering as many supplies as possible either before or during the siege.

Batter/Rebuild: The Attacker batters away at the Defender's stronghold. With luck, one or more sections of the stronghold will be breached, making it easier to attack. The Defender counters this by organising working parties to repair as much of the damage as possible.

Tunnel/Counter-tunnel: The Attacker builds underground tunnels that will allow at least part of their army to emerge inside the Defender's stronghold. The Defender counters this by building tunnels that intercept the Attacker's army while they are still underground.

SIEGE FOCUS

Both the Attacker and the Defender must choose 1 of the 3 siege tactics on which to concentrate their efforts.

To do so, each player secretly picks a number by hiding a dice behind their hand. The Attacker must pick a number from 1 to 3, and the Defender must pick a number from 4 to 6.

Once both players have chosen their numbers, the dice are revealed and the numbers cross-referenced on the siege table below. The siege table will say what modifiers, if any, will apply to the effects of the siege.

For example, if the Attacker chooses to concentrate upon starving the Defender's army and the Defender decides to focus on counter-tunnelling, the Attacker would add 1 to their Starve roll and subtract 2 from their Tunnel roll.

SIEGE EFFECTS

Next, the Attacker rolls to determine the effect of their siege methods on the Defender. Make all of the Starve rolls first, then the Batter rolls, and finally the Tunnel rolls.

Starve: The Attacker rolls a dice for each unit in the Defender's army, subtracting 1 from the roll if that unit is a **Hero** and applying any of the relevant modifiers from the siege table. On a 5+, that unit suffers D3 mortal wounds.

Batter: The Attacker rolls a dice for each terrain feature in the Defender's territory, applying any of the relevant modifiers from the siege table. On a 5+, that terrain feature has been breached, and none of its abilities can be used in the battle (it can still provide cover).

Tunnel: The Attacker and the Defender each roll a dice, and the Attacker applies any of the relevant modifiers from the siege table to their roll (the Defender's dice roll is never modified).

If the Attacker's roll is higher than the Defender's roll, they have successfully completed their tunnels and can pick 1 friendly **Hero** and 2 other friendly units to enter them (none of the units can contain **Monsters** or **War Machines** that have a Wounds characteristic of 8 or more).

Any units sent into the tunnels are removed from the battlefield and placed to one side. At the start of any of their movement phases, the Attacker can say that the units will emerge from the tunnels. The Attacker must pick a point within the Defender's territory to be the tunnel exit. The units using the tunnels must then be set up wholly within 6" of this point and more than 3" from any enemy units. This counts as their move for that movement phase.

THE ASSAULT

Once all of the siege effects have been rolled for, the Attacker commences their assault and the first battle round begins.

SIEGE TABLE

Defender's Counter-tactic	Attacker's Main Siege Method		
	Starve (1)	Batter (2)	Tunnel (3)
Gather Supplies (4)	-1 Starve	+1 Batter -1 Starve	+2 Tunnel -1 Starve
Rebuild (5)	+1 Starve -1 Batter	-1 Batter	+2 Tunnel -1 Batter
Counter-tunnel (6)	+1 Starve -2 Tunnel	+1 Batter -2 Tunnel	-2 Tunnel

SIEGE COMMAND ABILITIES

You can use the following command abilities in battles that use the Siege Warfare rules. The Attacker's command abilities can only be used by the attacking army, and the Defender's command abilities can only be used by the defending army.

ATTACKER'S COMMAND ABILITIES

Cry Havoc!: *Warriors are ordered to attack, no matter the cost.*

You can use this command ability in the combat phase. If you do so, pick 1 friendly unit within 6" of a friendly **Hero** or within 12" of your general. For the rest of that combat phase, add 1 to hit rolls and subtract 1 from save rolls for that unit.

Blastpowder Charges: *Explosives are rigged on command and used to shatter enemy fortifications.*

You can use this command ability in your hero phase. If you do so, pick 1 friendly unit within 6" of a friendly **Hero** or within 12" of your general. Then, pick 1 terrain feature within 3" of that unit. Roll a dice for each enemy unit garrisoning that terrain feature. On a 4+, that enemy unit suffers D3 mortal wounds.

Reinforcements: *Fresh troops arrive to join the battle.*

You can use this command ability in your hero phase. If you do so, roll a dice. On a 4+, pick 1 friendly unit that has been destroyed during the battle. You can set that unit up again wholly within 6" of the battlefield edge and more than 9" from any enemy models. This counts as that unit's move for the following movement phase.

DEFENDER'S COMMAND ABILITIES

Boiling Oil: *Sizzling hot oil is poured upon the attacking troops below.*

You can use this command ability in your hero phase. If you do so, pick 1 terrain feature that is garrisoned by a friendly **Hero** and at least 5 other friendly models. Roll a dice for each enemy unit within 3" of that terrain feature. On a 4+, that enemy unit suffers D3 mortal wounds.

Sally Forth: *A hidden gateway is opened, allowing the defenders to mount a counter-attack.*

You can use this command ability in your hero phase. If you do so, pick 1 terrain feature that is garrisoned by a friendly **Hero**. You can re-roll charge rolls in the following charge phase for any units that leave that terrain feature this turn.

Take Cover: *Troops are ordered to make maximum use of any cover available to them.*

You can use this command ability in the combat phase. If you do so, pick 1 friendly unit within 6" of a friendly **Hero** or within 12" of your general. For the rest of that phase, add 1 to save rolls for that unit and subtract 1 from hit rolls for attacks that target that unit.

SIEGE WARFARE ALLEGIANCE ABILITIES

This section contains new allegiance abilities available to the factions of each Grand Alliance in Siege Warfare battles. For each faction, there are Attacker- and Defender-specific abilities. The Attacker-specific abilities can only be used by the attacking army, and the Defender-specific abilities can only be used by the defending army.

CHAOS

BEASTS OF CHAOS
Attacker: If you have a Beasts of Chaos army, add 1 to Starve rolls in the siege phase.

Defender: If you have a Beasts of Chaos army, once per battle, you can use the Sally Forth Defender's command ability without spending any command points.

BLADES OF KHORNE
Attacker: If you have a Khorne army, once per battle, you can use the Cry Havoc! Attacker's command ability without spending any command points.

Defender: If you have a Khorne army, subtract 1 from Starve rolls in the siege phase.

DISCIPLES OF TZEENTCH
Attacker: If you have a Tzeentch army, at the start of the first battle round, after determining who has the first turn, you can remove 1 friendly **Tzeentch** unit from the battlefield and set it up again (any restrictions in the set-up instructions for the battleplan being used still apply).

Defender: If you have a Tzeentch army, subtract 1 from Batter rolls in the siege phase.

HEDONITES OF SLAANESH
Attacker: If you have a Slaanesh army, after armies have been set up but before the first battle round begins, friendly **Slaanesh** units can move up to 4".

Defender: If you have a Slaanesh army, once per battle, you can use the Boiling Oil Defender's command ability without spending any command points.

MAGGOTKIN OF NURGLE
Attacker: If you have a Nurgle army, in the first battle round, subtract 1 from hit rolls for attacks made with missile weapons that target friendly **Nurgle** units.

Defender: If you have a Nurgle army, at the end of each battle round, roll a dice for each enemy unit garrisoning any terrain features. On a 5+, that unit suffers D3 mortal wounds.

SKAVENTIDE
Attacker: If you have a Skaventide army, add 1 to your Tunnel rolls in the siege phase.

Defender: If you have a Skaventide army, once per battle, you can use the Take Cover Defender's command ability without spending any command points.

SLAVES TO DARKNESS
Attacker: If you have a Slaves to Darkness army, once per battle, you can use the Reinforcements Attacker's command ability without spending any command points.

Defender: If you have a Slaves to Darkness army, subtract 1 from Starve rolls in the siege phase.

DEATH

FLESH-EATER COURTS
Attacker: If you have a Flesh-eater Courts army, in the first battle round, you can re-roll run rolls for friendly **Flesh-eater Courts** units.

Defender: If you have a Flesh-eater Courts army, ignore the effects of any Starve rolls in the siege phase.

LEGIONS OF NAGASH
Attacker: If you have a Legions of Nagash army, add 1 to the roll made for the Reinforcements Attacker's command ability.

Defender: If you have a Legions of Nagash army, ignore the effects of any Starve rolls in the siege phase.

NIGHTHAUNT
Attacker: If you have a Nighthaunt army, ignore the effects of the Boiling Oil Defender's command ability on any friendly **Nighthaunt** units.

Defender: If you have a Nighthaunt army, ignore the effects of any Starve rolls in the siege phase.

OSSIARCH BONEREAPERS
Attacker: If you have an Ossiarch Bonereapers army, in the first battle round, add 1 to save rolls for attacks that target friendly **Ossiarch Bonereapers** units.

Defender: If you have an Ossiarch Bonereapers army, ignore the effects of any Starve rolls in the siege phase.

DESTRUCTION

GLOOMSPITE GITZ

Attacker: If you have a Gloomspite Gitz army, once per battle, you can use the Demolition Charges Attacker's command ability without spending any command points.

Defender: If you have a Gloomspite Gitz army, subtract 1 from Tunnel rolls made by the Attacker in the siege phase.

OGOR MAWTRIBES

Attacker: If you have an Ogor Mawtribes army, add 1 to Batter rolls in the siege phase.

Defender: If you have an Ogor Mawtribes army, subtract 1 from the number of mortal wounds inflicted on friendly **Ogor Mawtribes** units as a result of any Starve rolls in the siege phase.

ORRUK WARCLANS

Attacker: If you have an Orruk Warclans army, once per battle, you can use the Cry Havoc! Attacker's command ability without spending any command points.

Defender: If you have an Orruk Warclans army, subtract 1 from Batter rolls in the siege phase.

ORDER

CITIES OF SIGMAR

Attacker: If you have a Cities of Sigmar army, in the first battle round, add 1 to hit rolls for attacks made with missile weapons by **Cities of Sigmar War Machine** units.

Defender: If you have a Cities of Sigmar army, once per turn, you can use any Defender's command ability without spending any command points.

DAUGHTERS OF KHAINE

Attacker: If you have a Daughters of Khaine army, after armies have been set up but before the first battle round begins, friendly **Daughters of Khaine** units can move up to D6".

Defender: If you have a Daughters of Khaine army, once per battle, you can use the Sally Forth Defender's command ability without spending any command points.

FYRESLAYERS

Attacker: If you have a Fyreslayers army, add 1 to your Tunnel rolls in the siege phase.

Defender: If you have a Fyreslayers army, subtract 1 from Batter rolls in the siege phase.

IDONETH DEEPKIN

Attacker: If you have an Idoneth Deepkin army, in the first battle round, subtract 1 from hit rolls for attacks made with missile weapons that target friendly **Idoneth Deepkin** units.

Defender: If you have an Idoneth Deepkin army, once per battle, you can use the Take Cover Defender's command ability without spending any command points.

KHARADRON OVERLORDS

Attacker: If you have a Kharadron Overlords army, after armies have been set up but before the siege phase begins, you can remove D3 friendly **Kharadron Overlords** units from the battlefield and set them up again (any restrictions in the set-up instructions for the battleplan being used still apply).

Defender: If you have a Kharadron Overlords army, in the first battle round, add 1 to hit rolls for attacks made with missile weapons by friendly **Kharadron Overlords** units garrisoning any terrain features.

SERAPHON

Attacker: If you have a Seraphon army, friendly units returned to the battlefield by the Reinforcements Attacker's command ability can be set up anywhere on the battlefield more than 9" from any enemy models, instead of wholly within 6" of the battlefield edge.

Defender: If you have a Seraphon army, subtract 1 from Tunnel rolls made by the Attacker in the siege phase.

STORMCAST ETERNALS

Attacker: If you have a Stormcast Eternals army, do not take battleshock tests for friendly **Stormcast Eternals** units in the first battle round.

Defender: If you have a Stormcast Eternals army, once per battle, you can use the Sally Forth Defender's command ability without spending any command points.

SYLVANETH

Attacker: If you have a Sylvaneth army, add 1 to Batter rolls in the siege phase.

Defender: If you have a Sylvaneth army, once per battle, you can use the Take Cover Defender's command ability without spending any command points.

BATTLEPLAN
THE FALL OF KARHEIGHT

As the defenders of Karheight witness waves of undead warriors shambling through the Shyish arcway, they realise that they are looking upon slain comrades, raised from the dead by necromantic magic.

This unnerving discovery is accompanied by the howling of Nighthaunt spectres as they flood through the immense Realmgate, their focus on the destruction of every mortal in their path.

SIEGE WARFARE
Use the Siege Warfare rules from pages 70-72.

THE ARMIES
Each player picks an army as described in the core rules, and then they roll off. The player who won the roll-off picks which player is the Attacker. Their opponent is the Defender.

After the Defender has picked their army, they must split it into two contingents: the bastion and the garrison. There must be at least 1 unit in the garrison for every unit in the bastion (the army general can be in either contingent).

OBJECTIVES
Set up 2 objectives as shown on the map. One objective is located in the centre of the garrison area, and the other is located in the centre of the Defender's territory.

SET-UP
The Defender sets up their army first. They can only set up units from their bastion. Garrison units start the battle in reserve and will arrive during the battle (see The Garrison).

The Defender must set up their units anywhere wholly within their territory. The Attacker must then set up their army wholly within their territory, more than 6" from the Defender's territory. The territories are shown on the map.

THE GARRISON
Karheight's warriors rush to defend the barricades.

Starting from the second battle round, at the start of their movement phase, the Defender rolls a dice for each of their garrison units. On a 5+, that unit arrives on the battlefield. All of the models in that unit must be set up within 6" of the battlefield edge, wholly within the garrison area and more than 9" from any enemy units. This counts as their move for

that movement phase. Set up the unit before rolling to see if the next garrison unit will arrive.

WAVES FROM THE ARCWAY
Deathly energies spill from the Shyish arcway.

At the end of each battle round, the Attacker can call for additional troops and roll a dice. On a 4+, 1 unit will arrive on the battlefield. The Attacker adds either 1 unit of 2 or more models with a combined Wounds characteristic of 10 or less or 1 **Hero** or **Monster** with a Wounds characteristic of 8 or less to their army. Any units that arrive must be set up within 6" of the battlefield edge, wholly within the Attacker's territory and more than 9" from any enemy units.

BATTLE LENGTH
The battle lasts for 5 battle rounds.

GLORIOUS VICTORY
If one player controls both objectives at the end of the battle, that player wins a **major victory**. If the Defender controls 1 objective at the end of the battle, they win a **minor victory**. Any other result is a **draw**.

BATTLEPLAN
DEATHLY PURSUIT

Unable to withstand the Legion of Grief's ferocious assault, the defenders of Karheight are forced to fall back across the Corpse Wastes. Contingents of Nighthaunts are dispatched to scythe down the leaders of the retreating Chaos forces in order to prevent the hordes from regrouping.

THE ARMIES
Each player picks an army as described in the core rules. One player is the Survivors player. Their opponent is the Pursuer.

SET-UP
The Survivors player must pick 1 **Hero** from their army to be the Quarry, who will start the battle in reserve. The Quarry cannot be set up on the battlefield until their location has been revealed (see Find the Quarry).

The players alternate setting up units one at a time, starting with the Survivors player. Players must set up units wholly within their own territory, more than 12" from enemy territory. The territories are shown on the map.

Continue to set up units until both players have set up their armies. If one player finishes first, their opponent must set up the rest of the units in their army, one after another.

FIND THE QUARRY
The Nighthaunts' prey has taken shelter amongst the ruins of the Corpse Wastes. They must be rooted out and slain.

There are 3 points on the battlefield marked as hiding places. At the start of the Pursuer's hero phase, 1 friendly **Hero** within 1" of a hiding place can search it to see if they can find the Quarry.

To do so, roll a dice. On a 6, that hiding place is revealed to be the location of the Quarry and all other hiding places must be removed from the battlefield. Otherwise, the Quarry is not found and that hiding place must be removed from the battlefield.

If, at any point, 2 hiding places have been searched and the Quarry has not been found, the last remaining hiding place is revealed to be the Quarry's location.

If, by the start of the fifth battle round, the hiding place of the Quarry has still not been revealed, the players roll off (before any endless spells are moved). Starting with the player who won the roll-off, the players alternate removing hiding places from the battlefield, one at a time, until one remains. The remaining hiding place is revealed to be the Quarry's location.

Once the hiding place of the Quarry is revealed, the model must be set up within 9" of the hiding place and more than 3" away from any enemy units.

BATTLE LENGTH
The battle lasts until a player wins a **major victory** or for 5 battle rounds, whichever happens first.

GLORIOUS VICTORY
If the Quarry has not been slain at the end of the battle, the Survivors player wins a **major victory**.

If the Quarry is slain before the end of the fifth battle round, the Pursuer wins a **major victory**.

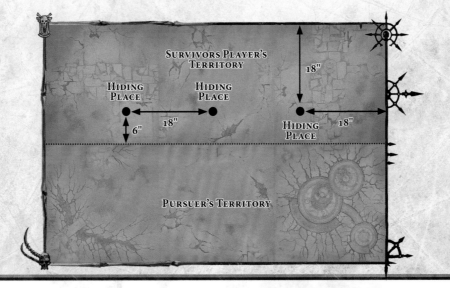

BATTLEPLAN
THE FOREST OF EYES

The Forest of Eyes is populated by millions of scuttling eight-legged horrors known as souleater spiders, creatures that feed not on flesh but on the spirit essence of their victims.

Even as the armies of Chaos and Death battle for control of the cursed wood, more of these hideous arachnids swarm around them…

OBJECTIVES
Set up 3 objectives as shown on the map.

SET-UP
The players roll off, and the winner decides which territory each side will use. The territories are shown on the map. The players then alternate setting up units one at a time, starting with the player who won the roll-off. Players must set up units wholly within their own territory.

Continue to set up units until both players have set up their armies. If one player finishes first, their opponent must set up the rest of the units in their army, one after another.

INFESTED OBJECTIVES
Souleater spiders spill from the corrupted earth in great swarms, falling over any who disturb them.

The value of the objectives changes in each battle round to represent the infestation of souleater spiders in the forest.

At the start of each battle round, before determining which player has the first turn, the players roll off to determine which objective is infested with souleater spiders. The player who won the roll-off then rolls a dice. On a 1 or 2, objective 1 is infested; on a 3 or 4, objective 2 is infested; and on a 5 or 6, objective 3 is infested.

After determining which objective is infested, the player who won the roll-off then rolls 2D6 for each unit within 9" of the infested objective. If the roll is equal to or greater than the Bravery characteristic of that unit, that unit suffers D3 mortal wounds.

BATTLE LENGTH
The battle lasts for 5 battle rounds.

GLORIOUS VICTORY
If one player has 1 to 4 more victory points than their opponent, they win a **minor victory**.

If one player has 5 or more victory points than their opponent, they win a **major victory**.

Any other result is a **draw**.

VICTORY POINTS
At the end of each battle round, the player controlling the infested objective scores 3 victory points.

If neither player controls the infested objective, the player controlling the most objectives scores 2 victory points.

If neither player controls the infested objective and both players control an equal number of objectives, each player scores 1 victory point.

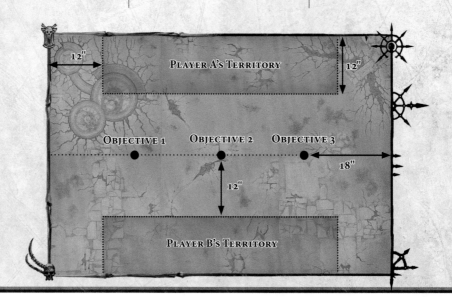

BATTLEPLAN
BRIDGE OF MOLTEN SCREAMS

The invaders push forward across a vital pathway known as the Bridge of Molten Screams, which stands guard over a river whose waters are composed of the tortured essences of the Everchosen's countless victims.

THE ARMIES
Each player picks an army as described in the core rules, and then they roll off. The player who won the roll-off picks which player is the Attacker. Their opponent is the Defender.

OBJECTIVES
Set up 1 objective as shown on the map.

SET-UP
The players alternate setting up units one at a time, starting with the player who won the roll-off. Players must set up units wholly within their own territory. The territories are shown on the map.

Continue to set up units until both players have set up their armies. If one player finishes first, their opponent must set up the rest of the units in their army, one after another.

LONG WAY DOWN
Far beneath the bridge rushes and roars a great river of tormented souls.

In this battle, the battlefield is divided into different sections to represent the bridge upon which the battle is fought. Units that cannot fly cannot move into the areas marked on the map as 'The Depths Below'.

COMMAND ABILITY
The Defender can use the following extra command ability in this battle.

Defiant Until the Last: *Stubborn is too kind a word to describe these grizzled warriors.*

You can use this command ability in your hero phase. If you do so, pick 1 friendly unit wholly within 12" of a friendly **Hero**. Until the start of your next hero phase, you can re-roll save rolls for attacks that target that unit. In addition, do not take battleshock tests for that unit until the start of your next hero phase.

CEASELESS ASSAULT
The deadly momentum of the Ossiarch assault does not relent.

At the end of each battle round, the Attacker can call for additional troops and roll a dice. On a 5+, 1

unit will arrive on the battlefield. The Attacker adds either 1 unit of 2 or more models with a combined Wounds characteristic of 10 or less or 1 **Hero** or **Monster** with a Wounds characteristic of 8 or less to their army. Any units that arrive must be set up within 6" of the battlefield edge, wholly within the Attacker's territory as shown on the map and more than 9" from any enemy units.

BATTLE LENGTH
The battle lasts for 4 battle rounds.

GLORIOUS VICTORY
The player with the most victory points at the end of the fourth battle round wins a **major victory**. If the players are tied on victory points at the end of the battle, the player with the most models within 6" of the objective wins a **minor victory**. Otherwise, the battle is a **draw**.

VICTORY POINTS
At the end of each of their turns, the player controlling the objective scores a number of victory points equal to the number of the current battle round. For example, if a player controls the objective at the end of their turn in the third battle round, they score 3 victory points.

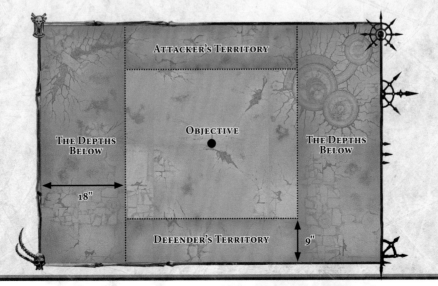

BATTLEPLAN
THE BATTLE OF HARADH'S TORMENT

An invading army has identified an ideal location from which to spring an ambush upon their foes. As the attackers march through the pass of Haradh's Torment, they fall victim to relentless volleys from enemy war machines. They must force a breach in their foe's line – or face obliteration.

THE ARMIES
Each player picks an army as described in the core rules, and then they roll off. The player who won the roll-off picks which player is the Attacker. Their opponent is the Defender.

OBJECTIVES
Set up 1 objective as shown on the map.

SET-UP
The players alternate setting up units one at a time, starting with the player who won the roll-off. Players must set up units wholly within their own territory, more than 12" from enemy territory. The territories are shown on the map.

Continue to set up units until both players have set up their armies.

If one player finishes first, their opponent must set up the rest of the units in their army, one after another.

VALLEY OF DEATH
The attacking army must traverse a narrow mountain pass, restricting their movement.

In this battle, the battlefield is divided into different sections to represent the narrow pass of Haradh's Torment. Units cannot move into the areas marked on the map as 'Impassable Terrain'.

COMMAND ABILITIES
The following additional command abilities can be used in this battle:

Pinning Volleys: *The defenders make use of the terrain's bottleneck and strategically placed war machines to overwhelm the foe with merciless volleys.*

The Defender can use this command ability in their shooting phase. If they do so, they can pick up to D3 enemy units on the battlefield and roll a dice for each unit. On a 4+, that unit suffers D3 mortal wounds.

We Must Break Through!: *Desperation forces the attacking army to overcome insurmountable odds to defeat the foe.*

The Attacker can use this command ability once per turn in their hero phase. If they do so, they can pick 1 friendly unit within 12" of a friendly **Hero**. That unit can make a normal move, but it cannot run.

BATTLE LENGTH
The battle lasts until a player wins a **major victory** or for 4 battle rounds, whichever happens first.

GLORIOUS VICTORY
The Defender wins a **major victory** if the attacking army is destroyed before the battle ends. The Defender wins a **minor victory** if there are no enemy units wholly within 12" of the objective at the end of the battle.

The Attacker wins a **major victory** if they control the objective at the end of the battle. The Attacker wins a **minor victory** if there are 3 or more friendly units wholly within 12" of the objective at the end of the battle. If none of the above conditions have been met at the end of the battle, the battle is a **draw**.

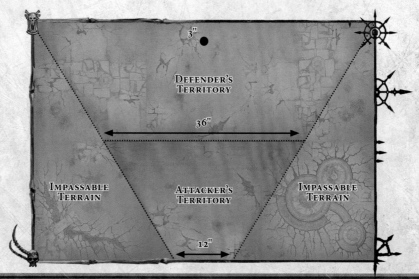

BATTLEPLAN
ASSAULT ON THE ARX TERMINUS

Playing into Katakros' hands, an army of the Eightpoints mounts a desperate attack against the formidable Arx Terminus.

Bombarded by siege engines and enemy missiles, they must push on and secure the walls, opening a path for their fellow warriors.

SIEGE WARFARE
Use the Siege Warfare rules from pages 70-72.

THE ARMIES
Each player picks an army as described in the core rules, and then they roll off. The player who won the roll-off picks which player is the Attacker. Their opponent is the Defender.

THE BATTLEFIELD
The Attacker picks 3 different terrain features in the Defender's territory to be siege targets.

Next, the Defender secretly picks 3 different terrain features anywhere on the battlefield to be treacherous defences.

SET-UP
The Defender sets up their army first. The Defender must set up their units anywhere wholly within their territory. The Attacker must then set up their army wholly within their territory. The territories are shown on the map.

SIEGE TARGETS
The besiegers attempt to destroy the fortress's deadly artillery and force breaches along its great walls.

A player controls a siege target when the terrain feature is garrisoned by friendly units.

TREACHEROUS DEFENCES
The fortifications of the Arx Terminus have been erected with cruel cunning to punish those who lay siege to it.

If an enemy unit finishes any move within 1" of a treacherous defence, the Defender can reveal that terrain feature to be a treacherous defence. If they do so, they must roll a dice for each enemy unit within 6" of that terrain feature. On a 4+, that unit suffers D3 mortal wounds. In addition, halve the Move characteristic of that unit until the end of the battle round.

BATTLE LENGTH
The battle lasts for 5 battle rounds.

GLORIOUS VICTORY
The Attacker wins a **major victory** if they control all 3 siege targets at the end of the battle.

The Defender wins a **major victory** if the Attacker controls 1 or none of the siege targets at the end of the battle.

If the Attacker controls 2 siege targets at the end of the battle, the battle is a **draw**.

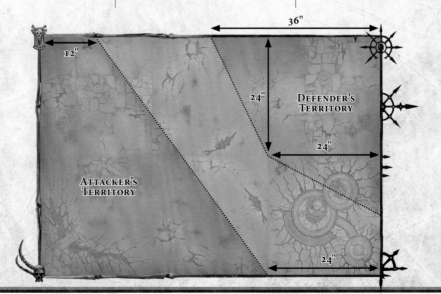

36"

12"

24"

DEFENDER'S TERRITORY

24"

ATTACKER'S TERRITORY

24"

BATTLEPLAN
ANGAZKUL-GREND

The forge-city of Angazkul-Grend is a sprawling centre of infernal industry. Its cursed factories arm the hordes of the Everchosen and provide daemonic siege engines for Archaon's ceaseless wars. By smashing the forge-city to rubble, Mortarch Katakros plans to deny his enemy a potent source of weaponry and armour.

THE ARMIES

Each player picks an army as described in the core rules, and then they roll off. The player who won the roll-off picks which player is the Attacker. Their opponent is the Defender.

OBJECTIVES

Set up 3 objectives as shown on the map. These will be referred to as 'Daemon Forges'.

SET-UP

The players alternate setting up units one at a time, starting with the player that won the roll-off. Players must set up units wholly within their own territory, more than 12" from enemy territory. The territories are shown on the map.

Continue to set up units until both players have set up their armies. If one player finishes first, their opponent must set up the rest of the units in their army, one after another.

REINFORCEMENTS

A centre of nightmarish industry for Archaon's legions, Angazkul-Grend is home to multitudes of daemonic nightmares.

At the end of each battle round, the Defender can call for additional troops and roll a dice. Add 1 to the roll for each Daemon Forge that the Defender controls. On a 5+, 1 unit will arrive on the battlefield.

The Defender adds either 1 unit of 2 or more models with a combined Wounds characteristic of 10 or less or 1 **Hero** or **Monster** with a Wounds characteristic of 8 or less to their army. Any units that arrive must be set up within 6" of the battlefield edge, wholly within the Defender's territory as shown on the map and more than 9" from any enemy units.

DAEMON FORGES

The smoke-spewing infernal forges of Angazkul-Grend conceal many threats.

If the Attacker controls any Daemon Forges at the end of a battle round, those Daemon Forges are razed and removed from the battlefield.

Each time a Daemon Forge is razed, the Attacker can return D3 slain models to each friendly unit on the battlefield. Set up any returned models within 1" of the friendly unit and more than 3" from any enemy models.

BATTLE LENGTH

The battle lasts for 5 battle rounds.

GLORIOUS VICTORY

If the Defender controls 2 or more objectives at the end of the battle, they win a **major victory**.

If the Attacker has razed 2 or more objectives at the end of the battle, they win a **major victory**.

Otherwise, the battle is a **draw**.

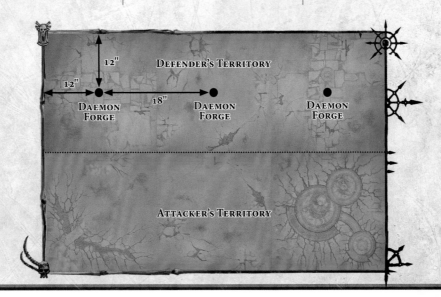

BATTLEPLAN
THE FATE OF THE EIGHTPOINTS

The threat of Mortarch Katakros has driven Archaon to set aside his campaigns of ruin. He has returned to the Varanspire to drive the enemy from his seat of power, the full might of the Dark Gods at his back. At the climactic moments of their first, fateful encounter, these military savants engage in single combat while their warriors kill and die around them.

THE ARMIES

Each player picks an army as described in the core rules, and then they roll off. The player who won the roll-off picks which player is the Invader. Their opponent is the Defender.

SET-UP

The players alternate setting up units one at a time, starting with the player who won the roll-off. Players must set up units wholly within their own territory, more than 6" from enemy territory and more than 6" from the area marked as 'Locked in Combat'. The territories and areas are shown on the map.

Continue to set up units until both players have set up their armies. If one player finishes first, their opponent must set up the rest of the units in their army, one after another.

LOCKED IN COMBAT

As the battle rages around them, the tyrants meet in single combat.

After armies have been set up, each player must pick 1 friendly **Hero** to be their champion for the battle. If either player's champion has a Wounds characteristic of 19 or less, that champion is treated as having a Wounds characteristic of 20 for this battle.

Set up both champions within 3" of each other at the centre of the Locked in Combat area. Only the champions can enter that area. In addition, the champions cannot be picked to be the target of spells, abilities, command abilities or attacks of any kind (friend or foe) made by any unit other than themselves or the enemy champion.

CHAMPIONS' ABILITY

Both champions gain the following ability:

Too Much to Lose: *With the weight of the realm on their shoulders, neither champion will easily suffer defeat.*

Roll a dice each time you allocate a wound or mortal wound to this model. On a 5+, that wound or mortal wound is negated.

In addition, if a rule for an ability or spell would cause either champion to be slain, that champion suffers D6 mortal wounds instead.

THE FINAL RECKONING

Each warlord knows that all will be decided by this final, climactic battle.

At the end of each battle round, each player adds up the Wounds characteristics of all enemy models that were slain during that battle round. The player with the higher total can heal D3 wounds allocated to their champion.

BATTLE LENGTH

The battle ends when one of the champions is slain.

GLORIOUS VICTORY

The Defender wins a **major victory** if the Invader's champion is slain. The Invader wins a **major victory** if the Defender's champion is slain. If both champions are slain at the same time, the battle is a **draw**.

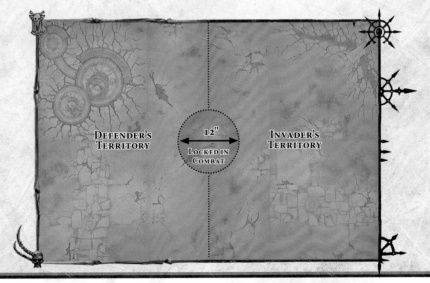

DEFENDER'S TERRITORY   12" LOCKED IN COMBAT   INVADER'S TERRITORY

HOSTS OF CHAOS

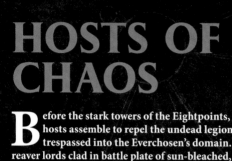

Before the stark towers of the Eightpoints, vast Chaos hosts assemble to repel the undead legions that have trespassed into the Everchosen's domain. Towering reaver lords clad in battle plate of sun-bleached, blood-spattered bone fight, slay and die alongside bile-spewing daemons and oiled, perfumed duellists in thrall to the God of Excess. Though these disparate allies share no kinship or loyalty, they have been fashioned into a force of destruction by the subjugating will of their master, Archaon, and a pure hatred of Mortarch Katakros and his Ossiarch Bonereapers.

These hosts hail from far and wide, and they are as varied in nature as the anarchic power of Chaos itself. Whether mortal or daemonic in origin, each boasts its own macabre customs and favours a unique and brutal style of warfare. Some are berserkers who overwhelm their foes in a thunderous explosion of pure violence, while others are masters of the swift cavalry strike or mayhem-loving wielders of maddening sorcery.

On the following pages, you will find an array of special rules that will allow you to bring these lethal hosts to life upon the tabletop. Allegiance abilities for the Legion of Chaos Ascendant provide everything you need to field a vast daemonic army united under the banners of all four Chaos Gods, including artefacts of power, spell lores and battle traits. Additionally, a number of warscroll battalions allow you to organise your force into deadly formations of daemonic champions, each with their own powerful abilities.

Also provided are rules and abilities for no fewer than thirteen Chaos hosts. These represent a variety of forces sworn to the Dark Gods, such as the elite Knights of the Empty Throne – a united force composed of Archaon's deadly Varanguard champions – and the Daemon Prince Be'lakor's dreaded Legion of the First Prince. All of these rules have been balanced and designed for use in your Age of Sigmar matched play games, so take to the battlefield and dominate your opponents in the name of the Dark Gods!

ALLEGIANCE ABILITIES

This section features two new sets of allegiance abilities for players fielding themed Chaos armies based around the Battle of the Varanspire: the Legion of Chaos Ascendant (pg 86-87) and the Knights of the Empty Throne (pg 90-91).

Each of these sets of allegiance abilities features new battle traits, command traits and artefacts of power. The rules for using allegiance abilities can be found in the *Warhammer Age of Sigmar Core Book*.

WARSCROLL BATTALIONS

These are formations made up of several Legion of Chaos Ascendant units that combine their strengths to gain powerful new abilities (pg 88-89).

HOSTS OF CHAOS

This section includes new allegiance abilities available to a Chaos army on the battlefield.

When you choose a Chaos army, you must decide which Chaos faction your army will belong to. You can then give it a Host of Chaos keyword from the following list.

For example, if you have chosen the Khorne allegiance for your army, you can give it the BALEFUL LORDS keyword. All KHORNE units in your army gain that keyword, and you can use the allegiance abilities listed for that Host of Chaos on the page indicated, in addition to the allegiance abilities they have for being from a Khorne army.

Khorne
- FLAYED (pg 92)
- BALEFUL LORDS (pg 93)

Tzeentch
- UNBOUND FLUX (pg 94)
- CULT OF A THOUSAND EYES (pg 95)

Nurgle
- MUNIFICENT WANDERERS (pg 96)
- DRONING GUARD (pg 97)
- BLESSED SONS (pg 98)
- DROWNED MEN (pg 99)

If you have chosen the Slaanesh allegiance for your army, you can give a GODSEEKERS HOST, a PRETENDERS HOST or an INVADERS HOST army the applicable keyword below:

Slaanesh
- LURID HAZE INVADERS HOST (pg 100)
- FAULTLESS BLADES PRETENDERS HOST (pg 101)
- SCARLET CAVALCADE GODSEEKERS HOST (pg 102)

Legion of Chaos Ascendant
- LEGION OF THE FIRST PRINCE (pg 103)

If a model already has a Host of Chaos keyword on its warscroll, it cannot gain another one. This does not preclude you from including the unit in your army, but you cannot use the allegiance abilities for its Host of Chaos.

THE LEGION OF CHAOS ASCENDANT

Woe betide all things – be they living or dead – when the Dark Gods set aside their ancient hatreds and unleash the full might of their daemonic hordes upon reality. The ground twists and the skies burn before the advance of the Legion of Chaos Ascendant, a force of utter desolation united under the eightfold mark of ruin.

When you are choosing a Chaos army, you can decide if it is a Legion of Chaos Ascendant army and has the Legion of Chaos Ascendant allegiance instead of another allegiance. If you do so, all units in your army gain the **CHAOS ASCENDANT** keyword. A Legion of Chaos Ascendant army can only include units that have the **CHAOS DAEMON** keyword.

BATTLE TRAITS - UNWAVERING DEVOTION

INFERNAL REALMWALKERS
The Legion of Chaos Ascendant is anchored to the material realms by the combined will of the Dark Gods.

You can roll a dice each time you allocate a wound or mortal wound to a friendly **CHAOS ASCENDANT DAEMON** unit. On a 6+, that wound or mortal wound is negated.

UNYIELDING LEGIONS
In battle, the Legion's overlords can call upon infinite reinforcements from their masters' domain.

At the end of your movement phase, you can pick 1 friendly **CHAOS ASCENDANT DAEMON HERO** that is on the battlefield and roll 3D6. On a 10+, you can summon 1 of the following units to the battlefield and

add it to your army. The unit that you can summon is determined by the **HERO**'s keyword as shown:

- **KHORNE HERO**: 10 Bloodletters
- **NURGLE HERO**: 10 Plaguebearers
- **SLAANESH HERO**: 10 Daemonettes
- **TZEENTCH HERO**: 10 Horrors of Tzeentch

The summoned unit must be set up wholly within 12" of that **CHAOS ASCENDANT DAEMON HERO** and more than 9" from any enemy units.

If the unmodified roll included any doubles, that **CHAOS ASCENDANT DAEMON HERO** suffers 1 mortal wound. If the unmodified roll was a triple, that **CHAOS ASCENDANT DAEMON HERO** suffers D3 mortal wounds instead.

COMMAND TRAITS - SCIONS OF THE RUINOUS POWERS
CHAOS ASCENDANT DAEMON HERO generals only.

D3 Command Trait

1 **Primordial Commander:** *This daemonic general has fought for the Dark Gods since time immemorial.*

If you pick this general to summon a sect of daemons for the Unyielding Legions battle trait, add 1 to the roll.

2 **Ruinous Aura:** *An aura of potent unreality surrounds this warlord.*

Add 1 to rolls for the Infernal Realmwalkers battle trait made for friendly **CHAOS ASCENDANT DAEMON** units wholly within 8" of this general.

3 **Infernal Charge:** *This warlord is an unstoppable force of destruction.*

You can re-roll charge rolls made for friendly **CHAOS ASCENDANT DAEMON** units wholly within 12" of this general.

ARTEFACTS OF POWER – GIFTS OF THE DEVOTED
CHAOS ASCENDANT DAEMON HEROES only.

D3 Artefact of Power

1 Fourfold Blade: *This blade is imbued with the power of the Chaos pantheon.*

Pick 1 of the bearer's melee weapons. If the unmodified hit roll for an attack made with that weapon is 5+, that attack inflicts D3 mortal wounds on the target and the attack sequence ends (do not make a wound or save roll).

2 Armour of the Pact: *This hellforged armour is granted to chosen champions of the Dark Gods.*

You can re-roll save rolls for attacks made with melee weapons that target the bearer.

3 Saintskin Banner: *This standard is woven from the flayed skins of priests and holy warriors.*

Subtract 1 from the Bravery characteristic of enemy units while they are within 9" of the bearer.

SPELL LORE – LORE OF RUINOUS SORCERY
You can choose or roll for one of the following spells for each **WIZARD** in a Legion of Chaos Ascendant army.

D3 Spell

1 Bolt of Ruin: *A searing missile of anarchic disruption blasts the target to ash.*

Bolt of Ruin has a casting value of 7. If successfully cast, pick 1 enemy unit within 18" of the caster that is visible to them and roll a dice. If the roll is lower than the number of models in that unit, that unit suffers D3 mortal wounds.

2 Echo of Hatred: *This spell grants banished daemons one final burst of wrath.*

Echo of Hatred has a casting value of 7. If successfully cast, pick 1 friendly **CHAOS ASCENDANT DAEMON** unit wholly within 12" of the caster and visible to them. Until the end of the battle round, if a model from that unit is slain by an attack made with a melee weapon, that model can fight before it is removed from play.

3 Spirit Gouge: *The caster rends the souls of the dead.*

Spirit Gouge has a casting value of 7. If successfully cast, pick 1 enemy unit within 12" of the caster and visible to them. If that unit has the **DEATH** keyword, you can re-roll hit and wound rolls for attacks made with melee weapons by friendly **CHAOS ASCENDANT DAEMON** units that target that unit until your next hero phase.

WARSCROLL BATTALION
HOST OF RAGE

ORGANISATION

- 2-3 Chaos Ascendant Khorne Daemon Heroes

- 8 Chaos Ascendant Bloodletter units

ABILITIES

First Blood: *These raging daemons are ever the first to spill the enemy's lifeblood.*

You can re-roll charge rolls for friendly units from this battalion.

WARSCROLL	POINTS	BATTLEFIELD ROLE
Host of Rage	160	*Warscroll Battalion*

WARSCROLL BATTALION
HOST OF CORRUPTION

ORGANISATION

- 2-3 Chaos Ascendant Nurgle Daemon Heroes

- 7 Chaos Ascendant Plaguebearer units

ABILITIES

Plague-smeared Blades: *The blades of these daemons are rife with horrific contagions.*

If the unmodified hit roll for an attack made with a melee weapon by a friendly unit from this battalion is 6, add 1 to the damage inflicted by that attack.

WARSCROLL	POINTS	BATTLEFIELD ROLE
Host of Corruption	180	*Warscroll Battalion*

WARSCROLL BATTALION
HOST OF THE ARCANE

ORGANISATION

- 2-3 CHAOS ASCENDANT TZEENTCH DAEMON HEROES
- 9 CHAOS ASCENDANT HORRORS OF TZEENTCH units

ABILITIES
Agents of the Change God: *Wielding the darkest sorceries, these daemons ensure the plans of Tzeentch are brought to fruition.*

Add 1 to casting, unbinding and dispelling rolls made for friendly **CHAOS ASCENDANT DAEMON WIZARDS** from this battalion while they are wholly within 9" of 2 or more other friendly units from the same battalion.

WARSCROLL	POINTS	BATTLEFIELD ROLE
Host of the Arcane	120	Warscroll Battalion

WARSCROLL BATTALION
HOST OF THE DEPRAVED

ORGANISATION

- 2-3 CHAOS ASCENDANT SLAANESH DAEMON HEROES
- 6 CHAOS ASCENDANT DAEMONETTE units

ABILITIES
Sadistic Exemplars: *The cruel sadism of these daemons has gained the favour of the Dark Prince.*

Add 1 to wound rolls for attacks made with melee weapons by friendly units from this battalion if they made a charge move in the same turn.

WARSCROLL	POINTS	BATTLEFIELD ROLE
Host of the Depraved	120	Warscroll Battalion

THE KNIGHTS OF THE EMPTY THRONE

Archaon maintains an inner circle of lieutenants chosen from amongst the dread ranks of the Eight Circles of the Varanguard. Known as the Knights of the Empty Throne, these ruinous champions are tasked with overseeing the Everchosen's endless conquests, an unholy mission they carry out with brutal efficiency.

When you are choosing a Slaves to Darkness army, you can decide if it is a Knights of the Empty Throne army and has the Knights of the Empty Throne allegiance instead of another allegiance. If you do so, all units in your army gain the **Knights of the Empty Throne** keyword.

BATTLE TRAITS – THUNDER OF OBLIVION

FISTS OF THE EVERCHOSEN
The Knights of the Empty Throne are amongst the most ruinous champions of the Dark Gods, charged with carrying out Archaon's tyrannical commands in the Everchosen's absence.

If you have given your army the **Knights of the Empty Throne** keyword, friendly **Knights of the Empty Throne Varanguard** units gain the **Hero** keyword if **Archaon** is not part of your army.

A **Knights of the Empty Throne Varanguard** unit with the **Hero** keyword can only have the command traits or artefacts of power listed opposite.

The Look Out, Sir! rule does not apply to **Knights of the Empty Throne Varanguard** units with the **Hero** keyword.

COMMAND ABILITIES
Unmatched Conquerors: *At Archaon's command, the champions of the Varanguard raze their enemy's strongholds to the ground.*

You can use this command ability at the end of your charge phase. If you do so, pick 1 enemy unit that controls an objective and is within 12" of a friendly **Knights of the Empty Throne Hero**. Roll a number of dice equal to the number of models in that unit. For each 3+, until the end of the battle round, the number of models in that unit that are counted when determining control of that objective is reduced by 1. The same unit cannot be affected by this command ability more than once per turn.

Failure is Not an Option: *The Varanguard will not stop until they have fulfilled their dark lord's commands.*

You can use this command ability when a friendly **Knights of the Empty Throne Varanguard** unit is destroyed. If you do so, roll a dice. On a 5+, a new **Knights of the Empty Throne Varanguard** unit of 3 models is added to your army. Set up the new unit wholly within 6" of the battlefield edge and more than 9" from any enemy units. You cannot use this command ability more than once per phase.

COMMAND TRAITS – OVERLORDS OF CHAOS
KNIGHTS OF THE EMPTY THRONE Varanguard generals only.

D3 Command Trait

1 Annihilating Charge: *This warlord is a master of the all-out assault.*

You can re-roll charge rolls for friendly KNIGHTS OF THE EMPTY THRONE units wholly within 12" of this general.

2 Inescapable Doom: *None can evade the wrath of this warlord.*

Enemy units within 3" of this general cannot retreat.

3 Wall of Cursed Iron: *The shields of this warlord's companions are all but impervious to conventional attacks.*

When friendly KNIGHTS OF THE EMPTY THRONE units wholly within 12" of this general use their Warpsteel Shields ability, add 1 to the roll.

ARTEFACTS OF POWER – CHAOS-TOUCHED TREASURES
KNIGHTS OF THE EMPTY THRONE Varanguard Heroes only.

D3 Artefact of Power

1 Flask of Daemonblood: *This flask is filled with the ichor of daemonic beasts. Consuming it grants the imbiber a portion of their unnatural resilience.*

In your hero phase, you can roll a dice for the unit bearing this artefact. If you do so, on a 4+, you can heal D3 wounds allocated to that unit.

2 Grasping Plate: *This armour is covered in writhing tentacles that reach out and ensnare nearby foes.*

The unit bearing this artefact is eligible to fight in the combat phase if it is within 6" of an enemy unit instead of 3", and it can move an extra 3" when it piles in.

3 Corrupted Nullstone: *This cursed stone devours magic.*

Once per battle, the unit bearing this artefact can attempt to unbind 1 spell in the same manner as a WIZARD. If it does so, that spell is automatically unbound (do not roll 2D6).

THE FLAYED

The Flayed are a warrior tribe of deranged killers who exult in the ruination of their enemies and the taking of trophies from their mutilated remains. When they enter battle, their bone armour – crafted from the skeletons of those they have butchered – soon becomes drenched in crimson gore.

Long has the Bloodbound Warhorde known as The Flayed haunted the wilds of the Eightpoints, preying upon the armies of the Everchosen and anyone else foolish enough to enter that benighted land. They make their camps in the Ruinscar Plains west of the Varanspire, a land plagued by a horrific variety of blood-hungry predators, among them corpse-dwelling meatwasps, thorned ravagers, rogue Slaughterbrutes and countless other horrors. It is a place where the baleful influence of the Blood God holds sway, suffusing every speck of land with boiling rage.

As well as hunting the Chaos-twisted fauna of their homeland, The Flayed often accompany the infernal legions of the Everchosen to war, following Archaon's forces through the great arcways to ravage and despoil distant lands. They also prey upon fellow worshippers of the Dark Gods, slaughtering isolated warbands and using the bones of their most memorable kills to craft their ivory armour. This process is a sacred act to the warriors of the Warhorde. They carve harsh runes into the osseous surface of their battle plate, marking the manner in which they acquired each bone. It is believed that when splattered with the fresh blood of their foes, these ritual markings channel the wrath of Khorne and imbue the bearer with fearsome resilience and strength.

ABILITIES

Blood-woken Runes: *When the bone armour of The Flayed is drenched in gore, Khornate runes carved into the surface blaze with power, imbuing these warriors with daemonic resilience.*

At the end of the combat phase, if any enemy **HEROES** or **MONSTERS** were slain by attacks made by a friendly **FLAYED MORTAL** unit in that phase, you can add 1 to save rolls for attacks that target that unit for the rest of the battle. A unit cannot benefit from this ability more than once per battle.

COMMAND ABILITY

Wrathspeaker: *In battle, this warlord speaks in an ancient daemonic tongue that inspires terrible wrath.*

You can use this command ability at the start of the combat phase. If you do so, pick 1 friendly **FLAYED MORTAL** unit wholly within 12" of a friendly **FLAYED MORTAL HERO** with this command ability. Add 1 to hit rolls for attacks made with melee weapons by that unit if it made a charge move in the same turn.

COMMAND TRAIT

A **FLAYED** general must have this command trait.

Vessel of Butchery: *The mere presence of this warlord seems to draw the eye of the Blood God.*

You can re-roll prayer rolls of 1 for friendly **FLAYED PRIESTS** wholly within 8" of this general.

ARTEFACT OF POWER

The first **FLAYED HERO** to receive an artefact of power must be given the Slaughterhelm.

The Slaughterhelm: *This horned battle-helm has been carved from the skull of a Slaughterbrute, and it is imbued with the dead monstrosity's insatiable bloodlust.*

Add 2 to charge rolls for the bearer.

THE BALEFUL LORDS

Clad in armour of midnight black, the Bloodthirsters of the Baleful Lords pounce upon their foes, tearing them limb from limb in a frenzy of carnage. These nightmarish champions are veterans of Khorne's endless wars in the Realm of Chaos, and they relish the opportunity to lay waste to the lands of mortals.

The Great Game fought between the Ruinous Powers is most violently contested across the roiling landscape of the Realm of Chaos, where sulphurous daemon hosts clash in battles of unthinkable scale and violence. The Baleful Lords are an elite daemon legion led by Bloodthirster generals who, through acts of particular brutality, have distinguished themselves in these bloody campaigns. As a reward, the Blood God has granted them the opportunity to wreak terrible havoc upon the Mortal Realms, and this they gladly do, carving a bloody gouge across the realms and butchering mortal warriors by the thousand.

The black-armoured Baleful Lords pick only the most prestigious targets, descending upon them with terrifying swiftness and ripping them apart with axe, whip and claw. The very havoc they wreak seems to empower these greater daemons and their infernal footsoldiers, strengthening their connection to the physical realms and allowing them to manifest outside the Blood God's domain for far longer than others of their kind. The sight of one Bloodthirster is enough to drive a man to madness – to face a pack of the creatures, competing against one another to commit the greatest feats of bloody slaughter, is enough to send even the most battle-hardened army fleeing in abject terror.

ABILITIES

Unbound Slaughter: *Bloodthirsters of the Baleful Lords delight in the opportunity to wreak terrible carnage upon the Mortal Realms.*

Friendly **BALEFUL LORDS BLOODTHIRSTERS** can run and still charge later in the same turn.

In addition, if you are fighting a Pitched Battle, you can include 1 additional Behemoth in your army, as long as every Behemoth in your army is a **BLOODTHIRSTER**.

COMMAND ABILITY

Frenzied Annihilator: *Lost in the throes of a murderous rage, this Bloodthirster ignores its wounds.*

You can use this command ability in the combat phase. If you do so, pick 1 friendly **BALEFUL LORDS BLOODTHIRSTER**. Until the end of that phase, when you look up a value on that model's damage table, that model is treated as if it has suffered 0 wounds.

COMMAND TRAIT

A **BALEFUL LORDS** general must have this command trait.

Thirst for Carnage: *Nothing can slow this warlord when they set their sights upon slaughter.*

Add 1 to charge rolls for friendly **BALEFUL LORDS BLOODTHIRSTERS** within 8" of this general.

ARTEFACT OF POWER

The first **BALEFUL LORDS HERO** to receive an artefact of power must be given the Black Brass Crown.

Black Brass Crown: *Fashioned from a sliver of the Blood God's own armour, this spiked crown is granted only to daemonic warlords that have won a great many victories for Khorne on the battlefields of the Realm of Chaos.*

Add 1 to save rolls for attacks that target the bearer.

THE UNBOUND FLUX

Spreaders of madness and mind-melting anarchy, the daemonic convocation known as the Unbound Flux makes war in a kaleidoscopic riot of flame and magic. Cavorting masses of daemons sweep forward in a roiling tide as cackling spellcasters hurl torrents of lurid and destructive sorcery at their foes.

Embodiments of Tzeentch's incomprehensible and bewildering nature, the Unbound Flux delight in displays of unbound sorcery – vibrant and colourful cascades of magic that sear the skin from their enemies' bones or transform them into gibbering piles of bubbling flesh. Madness is this convocation's sacred gift, one that they revel in spreading to all and sundry.

Whereas enchanted armour might protect against swords or even conjured flames, the mind boasts no such defence against the unravelling gaze of the Flux. Even their most humble arcane bolts and hexes are imbued with anarchic change of such purity that they can turn ordered thoughts to mayhem, bringing about self-mutilating derangement in those afflicted. Overcome by images of lurid, nightmarish surreality, such unfortunate souls will attempt to cleave open their own skulls or drive daggers into their eye sockets in order to free themselves from the Flux's mental onslaught.

Such is the powerful aura of pandemonium summoned by this convocation that it strengthens their connection to the material realms. It also grants their magical assaults extra potency, for the Flux's daemonic spellcasters thrive upon the terrible madness they inflict upon mortalkind.

ABILITIES

Maddening Cascade: *The spells of the Unbound Flux inflict self-destructive bouts of madness upon their victims.*

Each time a friendly **UNBOUND FLUX DAEMON WIZARD** casts a spell that inflicts any mortal wounds, roll a dice for each unit that suffered any mortal wounds inflicted by that spell. On a 4+, that unit suffers 1 additional mortal wound.

COMMAND ABILITY

Fuelled by Mayhem: *As the Unbound Flux transform the battlefield into a maddening nightmare, their daemonic sorcerers grow ever more powerful.*

You can use this command ability in your hero phase. If you do so, pick 1 friendly **UNBOUND FLUX DAEMON WIZARD** wholly within 9" of a friendly **UNBOUND FLUX DAEMON HERO** or wholly within 18" of a friendly **UNBOUND FLUX DAEMON HERO** that is a general. Add 1 to casting rolls for that **WIZARD** until the end of that phase. A unit cannot benefit from this command ability more than once per turn.

COMMAND TRAIT

An **UNBOUND FLUX** general must have this command trait.

Aegis of Insanity: *The air of unreality that surrounds the Flux strengthens their connection to the material realms.*

Do not take battleshock tests for friendly **UNBOUND FLUX DAEMON** units while they are wholly within 9" of this general.

ARTEFACT OF POWER

The first **UNBOUND FLUX HERO** to receive an artefact of power must be given the Enlightener.

The Enlightener: *A blow from this weapon floods the victim's mind with secrets of mind-blasting horror.*

Pick one of the bearer's melee weapons. If the unmodified hit roll for an attack made with that weapon is 6, that attack inflicts D3 mortal wounds on the target and the attack sequence ends (do not make a wound or save roll).

THE CULT OF A THOUSAND EYES

The Cult of a Thousand Eyes enact their intricate plans behind a veil of secrecy, planting their agents in the cities and strongholds of Order to pave the way for their incursions. When the fated hour dawns, these masked killers fall upon the bewildered enemy with ritual blades and bolts of eldritch magic.

The Arcanite Cults of the Disciples of Tzeentch are deeply embedded in every stratum of Sigmar's free cities, and none more so than the Cult of a Thousand Eyes. Using mind-leashing magic and spells of manipulation, this shadowy faction weaves its webs of intrigue across entire continents, sowing the seeds of treachery and corruption in preparation for the hour when its members will rise up and take their war to the God-King's oblivious masses. Nor are rival Chaos-worshippers immune to the Cult's machinations – the Thousand Eyes have infiltrated many of the Varanspire's savage war camps.

This exhaustive network of spies consists of many thousands of souls operating in discreet cells across vast distances, feeding a constant stream of stolen secrets back to their cabal of handlers. This flow of intelligence proves invaluable when the Cult must go to war, for they know their enemies' desires and plans intimately and delight in turning the tables on their foes with shimmering illusions, spells of mind control and other underhanded sorcery. Never has the Cult willingly approached a battle on an even footing with its opponents. Only when the enemy is lost in the throes of panicked disarray do the Thousand Eyes strike, dispatching their foes with contemptuous ease.

ABILITIES

Marked for Death: *Before battle begins, the Cult of a Thousand Eyes identifies the enemy's most powerful warriors and targets them for destruction.*

After armies have been set up but before the first battle round begins, pick up to D3 different enemy units. For the rest of the battle, you can re-roll hit rolls for attacks made with melee weapons by friendly **Cult of a Thousand Eyes Mortal** units that target those enemy units.

COMMAND ABILITY

Eyes Everywhere: *None can hide from the piercing gaze of the Thousand Eyes.*

You can use this command ability at the start of your hero phase. If you do so, pick 1 friendly **Cult of a Thousand Eyes Mortal** unit wholly within 12" of a friendly **Cult of a Thousand Eyes Mortal Hero**. Until the start of your next hero phase, enemy units do not receive the benefit of cover against attacks made by that unit.

COMMAND TRAIT

A **Cult of a Thousand Eyes** general must have this command trait.

Tzeentch is Pleased: *Whenever this warlord uses a cunning trick to throw their enemies' plans into disarray, they are granted the favour of the God of Sorcery.*

Each time you spend a command point, if this general is on the battlefield, you can roll a dice. If you do so, on a 5+, you can heal D3 wounds that have been allocated to this general.

ARTEFACT OF POWER

The first **Cult of a Thousand Eyes Hero** to receive an artefact of power must be given the Crown of Whispers.

Crown of Whispers: *This circlet of crystal whispers premonitions into the mind of the wearer, allowing them to react to danger with blinding speed.*

Add 1 to save rolls for attacks that target the bearer.

THE MUNIFICENT WANDERERS

One of Nurgle's most prolific Plague Legions, the Munificent Wanderers are responsible for sowing sickness and decay across vast swathes of the Eight Realms. This task they carry out with relentless good humour, for they believe that all who receive Nurgle's generous gifts are truly blessed.

The Munificent Wanderers have long earned the approval of their beloved Grandfather Nurgle, for no other Plague Legion has done such sterling work in proliferating his repulsive diseases. The Wanderers are led by the notoriously generous Great Unclean One Thrombolhox the Giving. Like their master, these daemons diligently ensure that their physical forms are infested with the greatest possible volume of Nurgle's foul gifts before striking out into the Mortal Realms. There, they spread the Plague God's blessings far and wide, so that none are left wanting.

The bulk of the Wanderers' ranks are made up of Tallybands of Nurgle formed of great mobs of Plaguebearers that shamble towards the enemy, shrugging off the most grievous wounds in their eagerness to share their bountiful foulness. Their unnatural flesh and rusted blades teem with parasites, plagues and poxes that they distribute vigorously and with cheerful relish. With every claw slash, every bite of rotted fangs, every liquid spray and sword thrust, they bestow the gifts of Nurgle on their unfortunate foes. Even when they are finally cut down, these daemons explode in a putrid eruption of bile and stinking blood, liberally splattering nearby enemies with a cocktail of unspeakable diseases.

ABILITIES

Locus of Corrosion: *With every step the enemy takes towards Nurgle's daemonic children, their weapons rust and corrode at an alarming rate.*

While an enemy unit is within 3" of any friendly **Munificent Wanderers Daemon** units, worsen the Rend characteristic of that unit's melee weapons by 1 (to a minimum of '-'). **Nurgle** units are unaffected by this ability.

COMMAND ABILITY

Infested with Wonders: *The Munificent Wanderers invite the most horrific and repulsive diseases into their flesh, and they cannot wait to share them.*

You can use this command ability in your hero phase. If you do so, pick 1 friendly **Munificent Wanderers Daemon** unit wholly within 14" of a friendly **Munificent Wanderers Daemon Hero** with this command ability. Until the start of your next hero phase, if an enemy unit ends a charge move within 3" of that unit, that enemy unit suffers D3 mortal wounds. A unit cannot benefit from this command ability more than once per turn.

COMMAND TRAIT

A **Munificent Wanderers** general must have this command trait.

One Last Gift: *Upon death, daemons of the Wanderers explode in a shower of putrid viscera.*

If the unmodified hit roll for an attack made with a melee weapon that targets a friendly **Munificent Wanderers Daemon** unit wholly within 12" of this general is 6, the attacking unit suffers 1 mortal wound after all of its attacks have been resolved.

ARTEFACT OF POWER

The first **Munificent Wanderers Hero** to receive an artefact of power must be given Mucktalon.

Mucktalon: *This sentient, daemonic blade seems to take great delight in biting into the flesh of enemy champions.*

Pick one of the bearer's melee weapons. Add 1 to hit rolls for attacks made with that weapon if the target is a **Hero**.

THE DRONING GUARD

The Droning Guard are a Plague Legion that excels in airborne attacks. Thrumming swarms of Plague Drones form the vanguard of their swift assaults, choking the skies with winged horrors and a stifling miasma that clots the very air to bring the foe to their knees.

The coming of the Plague Legion known as the Droning Guard is heralded by an immense storm of buzzing flies and a cloying stench powerful enough to sicken the most redoubtable of warriors. Not only does this horrendous miasma inspire great revulsion in the Droning Guard's enemies, it also masks the approach of the Legion's most potent champions. As the foe stumbles, retching and helpless, squadrons of Plague Drones spill from the clouds. These elite daemonic sky-riders crash into the thick of the fighting, laying about them with rusted blades even as their repulsive mounts put their mandibles and pus-dripping stingers to gruesome use.

It is no coincidence that Nurgle has bestowed the symbol of the plague fly upon the Droning Guard, for they are his most beloved aerial cavalry. Nurgle takes great pleasure in humming along to the atonal dirge created by the Legion's Rot Flies as they soar through the clotted clouds of his Garden. Indeed, such is his fondness that he has blessed both these creatures and their riders with a particularly grotesque resilience – the colossal daemonic insects have chitinous carapaces as tough as meteoric iron, while the swollen bellies of their Plaguebearer masters absorb any arrows or bullets loosed in their direction with sickening ease.

ABILITIES
Locus of Corrosion: *With every step the enemy takes towards Nurgle's daemonic children, their weapons rust and corrode at an alarming rate.*

While an enemy unit is within 3" of any friendly **Droning Guard Daemon** units, worsen the Rend characteristic of that unit's melee weapons by 1 (to a minimum of '-'). **Nurgle** units are unaffected by this ability.

COMMAND ABILITY
Twice-blessed Rotspawn: *Fortified by filth-encrusted carapaces and festering abdomens, the Rot Flies of the Droning Guard are oblivious to injury and ailment as they continue to spread their father's gifts.*

You can use this command ability in the combat phase. If you do so, pick 1 friendly **Droning Guard Plague Drones** unit wholly within 12" of a friendly **Droning Guard Daemon Hero** with this command ability. Until the end of that phase, add 1 to Disgustingly Resilient rolls made for that unit.

COMMAND TRAIT
A **Droning Guard** general must have this command trait.

Rotwing Commander: *This warlord leads the Rot Fly squadrons of Nurgle forth to swarm over the enemy.*

After armies have been set up but before the first battle round begins, friendly **Droning Guard Plague Drones** units can move up to 4".

ARTEFACT OF POWER
The first **Droning Guard Hero** to receive an artefact of power must be given the Cloak of Flies.

Cloak of Flies: *Formed from a writhing, droning mass of plague flies, this cloak whips outwards to intercept incoming strikes.*

Subtract 1 from hit rolls for attacks made with melee weapons that target the bearer.

THE BLESSED SONS

The Blessed Sons regard themselves as the greatest of Nurgle's mortal warriors, and they have good reason to make such a claim. No other Rotbringer army has battled so far and wide across the Mortal Realms or inflicted so many grievous defeats on the enemies of the Plague God.

Their bile-green battle plate emblazoned with the chitinous triptych of their brotherhood, the Blessed Sons lumber into battle, swinging slime-covered axes to hew their foes into bloody chunks. These bloated warriors delight in the enemy's revulsion and openly mock them as they slay, competing against one another to inflict the most gruesomely horrific wounds.

The Blessed Sons are not a single Contagium; rather, they are an elite brotherhood of many. Their ranks are too vast to be precisely counted, but it is estimated that the Sons number in the hundreds of thousands at the very least. This strength in depth has allowed them to bring war and disease not only to their familiar haunts in Ghyran but also to the fire plains of Aqshy, the monstrous wilds of Ghur and even several of the Shyishan underworlds. In time, the Sons believe they will conquer the realms entire in the name of Nurgle.

So numerous are the Blessed Sons' victories that they are notoriously arrogant; their generals are bloated not only with unspeakable corruption but with pride in their many revolting achievements. Their renown has led to them fighting alongside such luminaries as the Maggoth Lords and the brothers of the Glottkin, always to devastating effect.

ABILITIES

Nurgle's Embrace: *The bloated forms of these Nurglites are constantly at bursting point, ready to shower with virulent fluids any who dare strike them.*

Roll a dice each time a friendly **BLESSED SONS ROTBRINGER** model is slain in the combat phase. On a 2+, the attacking unit suffers 1 mortal wound. If the attacking unit has the **NURGLE** keyword, heal 1 wound allocated to that unit instead.

COMMAND TRAIT

A **BLESSED SONS** general must have this command trait.

Foul Conqueror: *This warlord is always driving their warriors on to new conquests in the name of Nurgle.*

Once per turn, you can use the At the Double command ability on a friendly **BLESSED SONS ROTBRINGER** unit within 12" of this general without spending any command points.

COMMAND ABILITY

Degraded and Defiled: *The Blessed Sons revel in the despair of their enemies, bludgeoning them with blighted blades and spiteful goading alike.*

You can use this command ability at the start of the combat phase. If you do so, pick 1 friendly **BLESSED SONS ROTBRINGER** unit wholly within 14" of a friendly **BLESSED SONS ROTBRINGER HERO** with this command ability. Then, at the end of that phase, pick 1 enemy unit that suffered any wounds or mortal wounds inflicted by that unit in that phase. If the combined number of those wounds and mortal wounds is greater than the Bravery characteristic of that enemy unit, that enemy unit suffers 3 additional mortal wounds.

ARTEFACT OF POWER

The first **BLESSED SONS HERO** to receive an artefact of power must be given the Blotshell Bileplate.

Blotshell Bileplate: *Crafted from the chitinous shell of a titanic Blotbeetle, this armour is all but impenetrable.*

You can re-roll save rolls for attacks that target the bearer.

THE DROWNED MEN

Stinking, piratical raiders who fall upon their foes with ferocious brutality, the Drowned Men are feared across the realms. They are masters of aerial and naval warfare, and the sight of their filth-encrusted sails upon the horizon is enough to strike dread into the most formidable warriors.

Clad in verdigrised copper, their bloated flesh dripping with foul-smelling brine, the Drowned Men are well named. They are the favoured Contagium of Gutrot Spume, the tentacled warlord who commands Nurgle's immense plague fleets. Specialists in naval and aerial combat, the Drowned Men sail across the oceans and skies of the realms in rotting and sorcerously infested hulks, searching for verdant new lands to despoil with disease. The Contagium prefers raiding tactics, striking from unexpected quarters and sowing as much sickness and death as possible before making their escape. Their warriors are surprisingly swift – at least compared to the lumbering pace usually displayed by the Plague God's soldiers. Hauling their swollen, stinking bodies over the side of a poxboat or plague blimp, they charge into battle with axes swinging before their foes have a chance to react.

Even by the standards of Nurgle's warriors, the stench that surrounds the Drowned Men is astonishingly foul: a blend of unwashed flesh and the acrid reek of dead fish left to fester in the sun. Their arms heavily muscled from manning filth-encrusted oars, the warriors of this Contagium also attack with terrifying strength, easily cleaving through iron breastplates and helms to shatter the bone beneath.

ABILITIES

Nurgle's Embrace: *The bloated forms of these Nurglites are constantly at bursting point, ready to shower with virulent fluids any who dare strike them.*

Roll a dice each time a friendly **DROWNED MEN ROTBRINGER** model is slain in the combat phase. On a 2+, the attacking unit suffers 1 mortal wound. If the attacking unit has the **NURGLE** keyword, heal 1 wound allocated to that unit instead.

COMMAND TRAIT

A **DROWNED MEN** general must have this command trait.

Bloated Raider: *This warlord favours the quick strike, overwhelming their foes with flights of hideous Rot Flies.*

You can re-roll charge rolls for friendly **DROWNED MEN PUSGOYLE BLIGHTLORDS** units wholly within 14" of this general.

COMMAND ABILITY

Kneel Before the Plague!: *The warriors of the Drowned Men are masters of their blighted arsenal, using their overwhelming strength to lay low their enemies while suffocating them with their deathstench.*

You can use this command ability at the start of the combat phase. If you do so, pick 1 friendly **DROWNED MEN PUSGOYLE BLIGHTLORDS** unit wholly within 12" of a friendly **DROWNED MEN ROTBRINGER HERO**. Until your next hero phase, if the unmodified wound roll for an attack made with that unit's Blighted Weapons is 6, improve the Rend characteristic for that attack by 1.

ARTEFACT OF POWER

The first **DROWNED MEN HERO** to receive an artefact of power must be given the Rot-kraken Hide.

Rot-kraken Hide: *This rubbery and appallingly foul-smelling jerkin of rot-kraken skin fits under the armour and is formidably resilient.*

Add 1 to the bearer's Wounds characteristic.

THE LURID HAZE

The Invaders known as the Lurid Haze announce their presence by unleashing great billows of suffocating, perfumed mist that sweep across the battlefield, concealing their movements and heightening every sensation. Striking from the midst of this intoxicating cloud, they indulge their every sadistic passion upon their foes.

Originally hailing from the misty canyons of the Ulguan Fadelands, the Lurid Haze are a band of sadists who roam the realms in search of the extreme sensations of battle. They heighten their senses even further with Prince's Skin, an incense made from the perfumed hides of their victims and a blend of forbidden ingredients: the tears of tormented prisoners, droplets of fragrant daemon blood and other repulsive and esoteric substances. When burned, this incense unleashes great gouts of sweet-smelling smoke that cover the land in a heady pall, enhancing their killing instincts while obscuring the enemy's vision. This practice has allowed the Lurid Haze to mask themselves from the retribution of both Malerion and Morathi, who have long sought to drive all Invaders from the Realm of Shadow.

Their minds and bodies raised to dizzying heights of sensation by the swirling vapours, the warriors of the Lurid Haze strike from the mist, eviscerating their quarry in an orgy of bloodletting before disappearing as quickly as they appeared. War leaders of the Lurid Haze often bear aloft censers filled with Prince's Skin, spreading the perfumed mist ever further and driving those warriors nearby into an exultant state that renders them all but immune to even the most lethal strikes.

ABILITIES

Billowing Mists: *The Lurid Haze unleash clouds of perfumed smoke to conceal their movements.*

After set up is complete but before the first battle round begins, you can remove D3 friendly **Lurid Haze Invaders Host** units from the battlefield and say that they are set up in ambush as reserve units (any set-up restrictions in the battleplan being used still apply). If you do so, at the end of your first movement phase, you must set up those friendly **Lurid Haze Invaders Host** units on the battlefield, wholly within 6" of the battlefield edge and more than 9" from any enemy units.

COMMAND TRAIT

A **Lurid Haze Invaders Host** general must have this command trait.

Feverish Anticipation: *Lurid Haze warriors cannot wait to glut themselves with the sensations of battle.*

You can re-roll run rolls for friendly **Lurid Haze Invaders Host** units that are wholly within 12" of this general when the run roll is made.

COMMAND ABILITY

Intoxicating Pall: *Immersed in the swirling vapours of their incense, warriors of the Lurid Haze find their reactions honed to a formidable edge.*

You can use this command ability once per turn in the combat phase. If you do so, pick 1 friendly **Lurid Haze Invaders Host** unit wholly within 12" of a friendly **Lurid Haze Invaders Host Hero** with this command ability. Until the end of that phase, add 1 to save rolls for attacks that target that unit. The same unit cannot benefit from this command ability more than once per turn.

ARTEFACT OF POWER

The first **Lurid Haze Invaders Host Hero** to receive an artefact of power must be given the Oil of Exultation.

Oil of Exultation: *This profane blend of unguents toughens the skin and heightens the senses.*

Add 1 to the Wounds characteristic of the bearer.

THE FAULTLESS BLADES

Followers of the Pretender warlord Zaresta Silverheart, the Faultless Blades are an order of Slaaneshi war-cultists who have dedicated themselves entirely to mastering single combat. They seek out only the most monstrous and deadly foes against which to test their perfection of the martial form.

Zaresta Silverheart, the Faultless One, is one of the most powerful Slaaneshi warlords in the realms, an utterly egomaniacal but undeniably fearsome duellist who regards herself as the greatest swordfighter in existence. Silverheart claims to be the only natural successor to the Dark Prince's throne. She has slain rampaging Maw-krushas, Sigmarite champions and even a mighty Bloodthirster of Khorne in single combat. In a long and bloody career, she has gathered a band of worshippers and daemonic admirers known as the Faultless Blades, who seek to emulate her deadly skill.

In order to prove their superiority, warriors of the Faultless Blades seek out only the most fearsome foes to pick apart in battle. They hunt bestial giants, deathly grave-lords and other horrors, delighting in the clash of emotions and sensations unleashed by a desperate duel to the death. For these obsessive souls, the most exquisite experience imaginable is to impale a foe's heart with the impeccably timed thrust of a sword or daemonic claw or to carve open a throat with a perfect backhand slice and feel the splatter of hot blood across their bare skin. Consumed with desperation to outdo one another, the Faultless Blades race to be the first to engage the fiercest enemy champions, gladly risking their own skin for a glimpse of eternal glory.

ABILITIES
Send Me Your Best: *The Faultless Blades desire to test their skill against the very deadliest of duellists.*

Add 1 to hit rolls for attacks made with melee weapons by friendly **FAULTLESS BLADES PRETENDERS HOST** units that target a **HERO** if that friendly unit made a charge move in the same turn.

COMMAND ABILITY
Armour of Arrogance: *These warriors refuse to acknowledge any wounds that their enemies inflict upon them, so sure are they of they own superiority.*

You can use this command ability once per turn in the combat phase. If you do so, pick 1 friendly **FAULTLESS BLADES PRETENDERS HOST** unit wholly within 12" of a friendly **FAULTLESS BLADES PRETENDERS HOST HERO** with this command ability. The first 2 wounds allocated to that unit in that phase are negated.

COMMAND TRAIT
A **FAULTLESS BLADES PRETENDERS HOST** general must have this command trait in addition to any others it has.

Contest of Cruelty: *Warlords of the Faultless Blades like to inspire fierce competition amongst their warriors to see who can score the most memorably gruesome kill.*

Friendly **FAULTLESS BLADES PRETENDERS HOST** units that start a pile-in move wholly within 12" of this general can move an extra 3" when they pile in.

ARTEFACT OF POWER
The first **FAULTLESS BLADES PRETENDERS HOST HERO** to receive an artefact of power must be given the Contemptuous Brand.

Contemptuous Brand: *This ebon blade has supped on the blood of countless kings, warriors and champions.*

Pick one of the bearer's melee weapons. Add 1 to wound rolls for attacks made with that weapon that target a **HERO**.

THE SCARLET CAVALCADE

Entirely obsessed with the sensation of speed, the deviant Godseekers of the Scarlet Cavalcade rampage across vast distances, scything through everything in their path. They believe that when they achieve their full and deadly velocity, they are blessed with brief glimpses of their missing god.

Led by the silver-haired deviant known as Reshevious and guided by the supernaturally enhanced senses of a mutated flesh-thing they call the Inhilus, the Scarlet Cavalcade have carved a trail of devastation far across the Mortal Realms, bringing death and horror to thousands in their ceaseless search for the absent Dark Prince. Masters of chariot warfare and quicksilver cavalry charges, the Cavalcade's elite riders attain the highest possible speeds before slamming into their quarry, exulting in the rush of sensation as gore drenches their armour and skin. No sooner has the enemy been slain than they follow the mewling cries of the Inhilus to their next destination.

The Scarlet Cavalcade prize lightning fast steeds – daemonic beasts that can outstrip a speeding arrow or master-bred racing mounts that can guide them swiftly and unerringly into the heart of the enemy ranks. Cavalcade riders often bedeck themselves with spurs and barbed hooks, which they use both to drive their mounts into a frenzied rampage and to skewer any foes who attempt to haul them from the saddle. The intoxicating, gory rush of a Cavalcade assault often draws forth blade-wheeled chariots and mounted daemonic riders from the Dark Prince's court, who revel in the carnage that the Godseekers leave in their wake.

ABILITIES

Excessive Swiftness: *Warriors of the Scarlet Cavalcade believe that by attaining a lethal velocity, they can commune with their absent god.*

At the start of your charge phase, if 2 friendly **SCARLET CAVALCADE GODSEEKERS HOST** units that each have 10 or more models are within 6" of each other, you can make 1 charge roll to determine the charge distance for both units in that phase.

COMMAND ABILITY

Vicious Spurs: *Cavalcade riders wear barbed spurs that can be used on their foes as well as their steeds.*

You can use this command ability at the start of the combat phase. If you do so, pick 1 friendly **SCARLET CAVALCADE GODSEEKERS HOST** unit that made a charge move that turn and is wholly within 12" of a friendly **SCARLET CAVALCADE GODSEEKERS HOST HERO**. Until the end of that phase, if the unmodified save roll for an attack that targets that unit is 6, the attacking unit suffers 1 mortal wound after all of its attacks have been resolved.

COMMAND TRAIT

A **SCARLET CAVALCADE GODSEEKERS HOST** general must have this command trait.

Embodiment of Haste: *This rider's fearsome speed is inspiring to all.*

You can re-roll battleshock tests for friendly **SCARLET CAVALCADE GODSEEKERS HOST** units wholly within 12" of this general.

ARTEFACT OF POWER

The first **SCARLET CAVALCADE GODSEEKERS HOST HERO** to receive an artefact of power must be given the Helm of the Last Rider.

Helm of the Last Rider: *The last heirloom of a ruined kingdom of horselords, this gilded helm radiates an aura of regal surety.*

Add 1 to the Bravery characteristic of friendly **SCARLET CAVALCADE GODSEEKERS HOST** units while they are wholly within 12" of the bearer.

THE LEGION OF THE FIRST PRINCE

The Daemon Prince Be'lakor is a being of ancient and malevolent evil who claims to have the favour of all four Chaos Gods. Be'lakor commands the Legion of the First Prince, a vast host of daemonic minions that he has led into battle countless times to crush empires and kingdoms to dust.

Be'lakor is a creature of shadow and terror, a manipulator who sows the seeds of doubt amongst his foes and watches them devour each other. His realms-spanning machinations are many, but there comes a time in all his plans when he must march forth and utterly destroy his enemies. It is then that he summons the Legion of the First Prince, his mailed fist. This immense host includes daemons of all shapes and forms, from the brazen shock infantry of Khorne's Bloodletters to the lithe and deadly Daemonettes of Slaanesh. All pay homage to the First Prince, who claims to be the first entity in all existence to gain the undivided favour of all four Chaos Gods. Such grand words have oft drawn the ire of Archaon the Everchosen, but Be'lakor's dominance over daemonic footsoldiers of every stripe cannot be questioned.

The Legion of the First Prince overwhelms the Daemon Prince's foes with a seemingly ceaseless tide of lesser daemons, each of them so throughly subjugated by the Dark Master's sinister will that they hurl themselves upon swords and arrows intended for him. Indeed, their numbers are so vast that when one is banished screeching to the warp, it seems as if another three take its place. When the First Prince takes to the field alongside this dread host, the enemy knows that their fate is truly sealed.

ABILITIES

First-Damned Prince: *Be'lakor claims to be the first entity to earn the combined favour of the Dark Gods.*

You can re-roll hit and wound rolls for attacks made by **Be'lakor** while he is within 8" of at least 1 of each of the following friendly **Legion of the First Prince** units: **Bloodletters, Plaguebearers, Daemonettes** and **Horrors of Tzeentch**.

In addition, before you allocate a wound or mortal wound to **Be'lakor**, pick 1 friendly **Legion of the First Prince Bloodletters, Plaguebearers, Daemonettes** or **Horrors of Tzeentch** unit within 8" of him and roll a dice. On a 4+, that wound or mortal wound is allocated to that unit instead.

COMMAND ABILITY

The Shadow Legion: *Be'lakor will throw waves of immortal servants at the enemy until they are crushed beneath the daemonic riptide.*

You can use this command ability once per turn at the end of the battleshock phase if **Be'lakor** is your general and on the battlefield. If you do so, roll a dice for each friendly **Legion of the First Prince Bloodletters, Plaguebearers, Daemonettes** and **Horrors of Tzeentch** unit on the battlefield. On a 3+, you can return D3 slain models to that unit.

SPELL LORE

Each **Wizard** in a **Legion of the First Prince** army knows the following spell in addition to any other spells that they know.

The Master's Command: *Invoking the will of Be'lakor the First Prince, the caster orders their daemonic warriors to fight on with relentless fury.*

The Master's Command has a casting value of 7. If successfully cast, pick 1 friendly **Legion of the First Prince Bloodletters, Plaguebearers, Daemonettes** or **Horrors of Tzeentch** unit wholly within 12" of the caster and visible to them. Until the start of your next hero phase, if a model from that unit is slain by an attack made with a melee weapon, that model can fight before it is removed from play.